Translating Emotion

Intercultural Studies and Foreign Language Learning

EDITED BY

Arnd Witte and Theo Harden

Volume 4

PETER LANG

Oxford · Bern · Berlin · Bruxelles · Frankfurt am Main · New York · Wien

Translating Emotion

Studies in Transformation and Renewal Between Languages

EDITED BY

Kathleen Shields and Michael Clarke

PETER LANG

Oxford · Bern · Berlin · Bruxelles · Frankfurt am Main · New York · Wien

Bibliographic information published by Die Deutsche Nationalbibliothek.
Die Deutsche Nationalbibliothek lists this publication in the Deutsche Nationalbibliografie; detailed bibliographic data is available on the Internet at http://dnb.d-nb.de.

A catalogue record for this book is available from the British Library.

Library of Congress Cataloging-in-Publication Data:

Translating emotion : studies in transformation and renewal between languages / Kathleen Shields and Michael Clarke, editors.
p. cm. -- (Intercultural studies and foreign language learning ; v. 4)
Includes bibliographical references and index.
ISBN 978-3-0343-0115-2 (alk. paper)
1. Translating and interpreting. I. Shields, Kathleen, 1959- II. Clarke, Michael, 1966-
P306.T6785 2011
418'.02--dc22
2010050647

ISSN 1663-5809
ISBN 978-3-0343-0115-2

Hochfeldstrasse 32, CH-3012 Bern, Switzerland
info@peterlang.com, www.peterlang.com, www.peterlang.net

Printed in Germany

Contents

Acknowledgements vii

KATHLEEN SHIELDS AND MICHAEL CLARKE
Introduction 1

FLORIAN KROBB
Emotions Contained and Converted:
Goethe's *Roman Elegies* and Translation 9

MICHAEL CLARKE
Translation and Transformation:
A Case Study from Medieval Irish and English 29

JOHN KINSELLA
East Meets West: Some Portuguese Translations of Eastern Poetry 55

CORMAC Ó CUILLEANÁIN
Channelling Emotions, Eliciting Responses:
Translation as Performance 67

KATHLEEN SHIELDS
Auditory Images as Sites of Emotion:
Translating Gerard Manley Hopkins into French 87

MICHAEL CRONIN
A Dash of the Foreign: The Mixed Emotions of Difference 107

MICHELLE WOODS
Love and Other Subtitles:
Comedic and Abusive Subtitling in *Annie Hall* and *Wayne's World* 125

Bibliography 145

Notes on Contributors 159

Index 161

Acknowledgements

The editors would like to thank the Maynooth translation studies group for their support in the initial stages of this volume. In particular we are grateful to the enouragement of Prof. Peter Denman at this stage. Thanks are also due to Sikorski Edition for kind permission to quote the short extract from David Fanning's monograph, *Shostakovich: String Quartet No. 8* (London: Ashgate, 2004) that appears in Cormac Ó Cuilleanáin's article. We are also grateful to the National University of Ireland and to NUI Maynooth for providing grants towards the publication of this volume.

KATHLEEN SHIELDS AND MICHAEL CLARKE

Introduction

This collection of essays can be situated in a development that has been underway in our field since the early 1990s, namely the increasing focus on translators themselves: translators as embodied agents, not instruments or conduits. The dominant, 'classical' paradigm of the Western tradition had involved an effacement of the translator's identity, an assumption underpinned by dualist theories of meaning. Was this simply because Bible translation provided the focus point for much of the thinking that was done in this area? Already, from the mid-1970s, descriptive translation studies brought about a significant change of perspective. Translations were no longer seen as finished products to be compared with the source text and potentially found wanting. Gideon Toury and others found rich material by studying the reception of translations in the worlds of their target languages, along with the behavioural norms implicated in the choices made by the translators.[1] In this context Douglas Robinson's book *The Translator's Turn* (1991) marks a shift from general patterns of translators' choices towards a focus on the person of the individual translator.[2] Robinson makes an appeal for 'a somatics of translation': in such a model, sense and meaning are grounded not only in cognition but also in bodily sensation. Pursuing the theme of embodiment, he calls for an awareness of what he terms the translator's 'limbic system' as opposed to 'mentalist categories'.[3]

1 See, for example, Gideon Toury, *Descriptive Translation Studies and Beyond* (Amsterdam: Benjamins, 1995); Theo Hermans, ed. *The Manipulation of Literature: Studies in Literary Translation* (London: Croom Helm, 1985).

2 Douglas Robinson, *The Translator's Turn* (Baltimore and London: Johns Hopkins University Press, 1991).

3 Robinson, *The Translator's Turn*, pp. x–xii.

As we consider the interplay between translation and emotion, it is perhaps suprising that we have found such a rich seam in the study of the political importance of translation – not just in terms of transmission of ideas, but also with regard to the changes in emotional state that can be brought about by cross-language transfer. In post-colonial and nationalist arenas, almost inevitably, translation does not bring about harmony and mutual understanding: it can also generate aversion and xenophobia, and even fruitful *mis*understandings.[4]

The essays in this book focus on different kinds of emotion and on different levels of the translation process: one examines the broad socio-cultural context, some focus on the social event enacted in translation, some on the translator's own performative act. Some, again, problematize the linguistic challenges posed by the cultural distance of the emotions embodied in the texts to be translated. Translators themselves are a central concern throughout the collection, which is perhaps why two of the essays take as their starting-point the question of translating love. Love, or explaining and understanding the other to oneself, becomes a trope in its own right, and cultural misunderstandings can give rise to disappointment and frustration.

Examining the question of emotion and translation necessarily involves what Daniel Simeoni calls the 'view from the agent', whether the agent is the translator or the scholar studying translations (and the general reader can also be included with the scholar).[5] In this way a range of possible questions arises. There is the practical matter of how to translate words from semantic fields that have to do with emotion. For instance, do you translate the Portuguese word *alma* in a text by Pessoa by *guts*, *heart*, or *soul*?[6] There

4 See, for instance, Maria Tymoczko, *Translation in a Postcolonial Context* (Manchester: St Jerome, 1999) and Vicente Rafael, *Contracting Colonialism: Translation and Christian Conversion in Tagalog Society under Early Spanish Rule* (Ithaca: Cornell University Press, 1988).

5 Daniel Simeoni, 'Translating and Studying Translation: The View from the Agent', *Meta* 40.3 (1995), 445–60.

6 See the discussion of this topic at http://poetry.about.com/od/oq/a/pessoa.htm. Accessed 14 August 2010.

may be a wide (unbridgeable?) gulf between the ways of conceiving of emotion that made sense in different cultures and at different times. It follows that different ways of conceptualizing emotions will lead to different ways of translating them – a concern that lies behind Michael Clarke's essay in this book on medieval Irish and Old English translation strategies. How do translators then carry out their work as cultural intermediaries? This is a case in point in John Kinsella's article on Portuguese versions of Chinese poetry. How does the translator's emotion manifest itself in an individual text or discourse? To what extent does the translator's background cause her or him to emphasize intellectual cognition and to play down emotion or affect? Where does emotion drive language choices that might appear on the surface to be purely cognitive? How does the translator create new texts that are likely to excite emotion in their receivers? Cormac Ó Cuilleanáin's essay on translation as performance examines this last question.

In the English-language context, the key to the semantics of emotion is often its contrastive relation to cognition. It is in this way that Andrew Chesterman uses the term, when he argues that models of translation causality must include the translator's subjectivity: 'Think-aloud protocols', where translators are asked to note down their thought processes as they work, 'provide information about *cognitive and even emotional causes*' [our italics].[7] Chesterman – and it is also the position adopted by the contributors to this book – makes the point that emotion must be included alongside cognition and that the two necessarily interact at various stages in the translation process:

> The causal paradigm does not focus exclusively on external causes, but also covers the affects of internal, subjective factors on translatorial choices. These can include very subjective factors like attitude, emotional state, personality, gender, even sexual orientation.[8]

7 Andrew Chesterman, 'Semiotic Modalities in Translation Causality', *Across Languages and Cultures* 3.2 (2002), 145–58 (149).

8 Andrew Chesterman, 'Semiotic Modalities', 151.

From the perspective of the scholar (and of the users of translations) both commonsense ideas about translation and more elaborated theories tend to favour cognition over emotion. There are at least two explanations for this. While translation studies began as a humanistic discipline and grew out of literary studies, hermeneutics and the study of meaning, it also has ambitions to be a social science with verifiable hypotheses and causal explanations. When translators are formally trained their subject is often perceived as analagous to engineering: translating is considered to be a transfer of cognitive content as opposed to, for example, a performance or an act. The most important part of semantic 'content' is perceived to do with communication of ideas, not feelings. Henri Meschonnic has attacked this way of thinking, which leaves out the kinesthetic, prosodic, ludic aspects of language.[9] Where does the semantic content requiring to be translated actually reside? Even in literary translation, despite the proliferation of metaphors that try to capture the subjective elements involved, it is the cognitive spirit that is seen as the most important thing to carry across into the other language, while the physical and emotional matter of the source language falls away.

The Romantic movement offers a challenge to this divide, as Florian Krobb's essay on Goethe shows. The translator, like the poet and lover, fuses the spiritual and the physical while appealing to universal values of human civilization. Goethe in his *Roman Elegies* anticipates his own concept of *Weltliteratur*, which he was to develop explicitly decades later. The history of the multiple translations of the *Roman Elegies* into English is itself undermining of Goethe's concept. The English translators are obsessed with metrical form while their concern for clarity leads them to iron out important ambivalences. Furthermore, they are limited by their own understanding of the purpose of the erotic in this work. All of these features run counter to a central feature of the *Elegies*: the healing of Babelian rifts through the creation of *Weltliteratur*.

Different ways of conceiving of emotions have existed in different cultures, whether these are viewed temporally or spatially. Michael Clarke's

9 Henri Meschonnic, *Poétique du traduire* (Paris: Verdier, 1999).

article explores the corpus of early medieval Irish texts in which Graeco-Roman heroic and mythological narrative is transformed under the characteristic styles and structures of native Irish saga. Clarke portrays these translations as an example of aggressive cultural self-assertion, absorbing the heroic past of Ireland and that of the Mediterranean world into a single narrative cycle with a single linguistic and imaginative register. A case in point is the language used to describe extreme emotional states, specifically the transformation of warriors in battle at moments of passion and frenzy. Examples show that the translators have subordinated the language and imagery of the source texts to those of the target language so fully that the product of the act of translation is indistinguishable from free composition as seen in narratives with indigenous subject matter.

Translations from Chinese present a more resistant challenge, as John Kinsella argues in his article on the Chinese translations of Azorean poet Emanuel Félix. From the beginnings of Jesuit involvement in China and Japan, there was an engagement with the Confucian concept of heart-mind or 'living up to one's word'. Chinese poetry is not 'other' but 'unfamiliar', and Félix's texts are a dialogue with the Chinese poetry of the particular. Kinsella concludes with his own experience of translating these Portuguese texts into English, in particular the challenge arising from cultural differences in expressing emotion.

Cormac Ó Cuilleanáin reflects on how translators can approach the task of transmitting emotional content and its effects. Translators are performers who are compelled to take personal ownership of the works they transmit, whether this is a song, a speech, or a written text. Pressure of personal feeling must be accounted for in the translated version if the text is to be counted as a communicative act. The essay ranges across different translation types – interlingual, intralingual and intersemiotic – as well as different media: song, gesture, spoken word and written word. The biographical resonances of the Shostakovich opera *Lady Macbeth of Mtsenk*, the emotional complexity of the Klezmer tradition, the rhetoric of Martin Luther King, the ambivalent roles of translator/interrogators at Guantánamo Bay, the sanitizing of violent emotions in translations of Psalm 157, all point to the moral duty that translators have, to transmit emotional elements even when these are questionable.

Auditory imagery is often put to one side under the old-fashioned heading of 'prosody', yet it draws on the irrational, emotional, ludic and arbitrary parts of a language, the parts that cannot be easily isolated into cognitive content. Kathleen Shields's essay argues that translating such images mobilizes powerful individual and collective beliefs and values. Examples include how to cope with puns in a neutral scientific genre, as well as the extreme challenge of translating Hopkins into French and the decisions made by one of his recent translators. The essay considers recent developments in translation studies, in particular the growing interest in the translator's subjectivity and unconscious, in order to make the case for giving a bigger place in the study of translations to pre-literate auditory imagery.

Daniel Simeoni (borrowing from Bourdieu) introduced the term *habitus* into translation studies, when he examined the inculcation of translators into the profession. This approach opens up many possibilities for the question of emotions in translation. Central to Simeoni's understanding of habitus is a synopsis by John B. Thompson in his introduction to Bourdieu's *Language and Symbolic Power*:

> The habitus is a set of dispositions which incline agents to act and react in certain ways. The dispositions generate practices, perceptions and attitudes which are 'regular' without being consciously co-ordinated or governed by any 'rule'... Dispositions are acquired through a gradual process of inculcation in which early childhood experiences are particularly important.[10]

In his work on language, Bourdieu tends to place emphasis on formal education and the education system as a whole in the process of inculcation. Yet there is also a case for studying informal education and the self-education of individual translators. In rapidly changing social and political environments, much of the most significant translating is done informally, on the job, as a sort of *bricolage* requiring invention and inventiveness.

10 Daniel Simeoni, 'The Pivotal Status of the Translator's Habitus', *Target* 10.1 (1998), 1–39. Pierre Bourdieu, *Language and Symbolic Power*, ed. John B. Thompson, trans. Gino Raymond and Matthew Adamson (Cambridge: Polity Press, 1997), p. 12.

Michael Cronin's essay examines just such an inventiveness in late-modern writing in Irish and English, where multilingualism in both originals and their translations bypasses the notion of loyalty to one language or another. Even during the early twentieth century the relationship between Irish and Hiberno-English was not as watertight as speakers wished it to be, not simply one of 'linguistic proximity and syntactic indebtedness'. The porosity between them has been taken further by contemporary writers such as Louis de Paor and Gabriel Rosenstock, so that the two languages (and others) echo across and within the texts and their translations. In late-modern Ireland this multiple language loyalty points to a reconfiguration that can be situated in the context of Ireland's 'incorporation into the turbomarket of the global English language'. Translation becomes more than simply the creation of an end product for a user who has no idea that he or she is receiving something that has been translated. Rather, in debates about multiculturalism as well as in literature and film, it has become a central mode of communication for this global age.

This point underpins the article by Michelle Woods. She studies the way translation itself can be used as a trope of an emotion, in this instance as a trope of love in contemporary film, and analyses how the interaction between moving image and text conveys emotion via translation. This can take place in different ways, for instance, through the use of subtitles for comedic effect as in *Annie Hall* (1977) and *Wayne's World* (1992). At a deeper level the subtitles point to a linguistically heterogenous society, since there is a constant need for translation not only between the sexes but also between socio-ethnic American backgrounds. Translation as an intralingual phenomenon reveals barriers and resistance to comprehension 'even in the act of declaring love'. To paraphrase Richard Sennett, the subtitles open up a public conversation about differences that cannot be resolved, a space in which people come together who will always disagree or who will never understand one another.[11]

11 See Richard Sennett, 'What is to be done?' [review of Tony Judt's book *Ill Fares the Land*], *TLS* 30 July 2010, p. 28.

This collection is broad in scope, spanning a variety of languages, cultures and periods as well as media and genres. The essays are unified in their approach to a topic rarely directly dealt with and they map out important areas of enquiry: the translator as an emotional cultural intermediary, the importance of emotion to cognitive meaning, the place of emotion in linguistic reception, and translation itself as a trope whereby emotion can be expressed.

FLORIAN KROBB

Emotions Contained and Converted: Goethe's *Roman Elegies* and Translation

Goethe and world literature

In the German context and beyond, Johann Wolfgang Goethe (1749–1832) is central to the debates on translation as practitioner and as theorist. This is not only because he was an avid translator himself, being amongst the first who attempted an early systematics of translational activity and purpose (in his *Noten und Abhandlungen zum West-Östlichen Divan* [Notes and Reflections on the West-Eastern Divan, 1819] and also in various other places), but also because he worked as a great totaliser, integrator and unifier in literature and in the sciences. In this way he promoted conditions in which translation could flourish.[1] The concept of *Weltliteratur*, a term of Goethe's coinage, encapsulates this notion of translingual human expression.[2] It is no coincidence that this term from then on provided the umbrella under which the attendant issues were discussed.

Goethe's famous pronouncements on world literature date from the late 1820s. For a variety of reasons this timing is significant. He starts to

1 The notes and reflections are printed in Johann Wolfgang von Goethe, *Das Problem des Übersetzens*, ed. by Hans-Joachim Störig (Darmstadt: Wissenschaftliche Buchgesellschaft, 1973), 34–7. For an English translation see André Lefevere, ed., *Translating Literature: the German Tradition from Luther to Rosenzweig* (Assen: van Gorcum, 1977), 35–9; Lawrence Venuti, ed., *The Translation Studies Reader* 2nd edn (New York and London: Routledge, 2004), 64–6.

2 David Damrosch, *What is World Literature?* (Princeton: Princeton University Press, 2003), 4–7.

ruminate about world literature shortly after his own most conscious and deliberate act of appropriating the most foreign of foreign literatures and the attendant reflections on translation in the *West-Östlicher Divan* of 1819. The pronouncements, furthermore, were sparked by Thomas Carlyle's English translation of Goethe's novel *Wilhelm Meister* and the continued exchanges about Carlyle's Schiller biography (1825) and his collection *German Romance* (1827). In other words they are connected to an instance of translinguistic and transnational literary collaboration. Arguably, Goethe's preoccupation with the concept and reality of world literature was related also to his concern for his own legacy. After all, he was just preparing the *Ausgabe letzter Hand* of his works which started to appear in 1827, the last edition designed and authorized by the writer himself, who was approaching his eightieth year. But even if Goethe's concern for the place of his name in the larger, supra-national scheme of things, that is in the canon of lasting *international* masterpieces, sparked the coinage and elaboration of the notion of world literature as late as the 1820s, Goethe's awareness of and engagement with a universal dimension of literary production date back to at least the 1780s when, between 1788 and 1790, he composed a cycle of poetry with a clear world-literary slant, the *Römische Elegien* [Roman Elegies]. Most of the poems were first published in 1795 in Friedrich Schiller's magazine *Die Horen*. These dates – from the 1780s to the end of the 1820s – also frame the very period of profound change in German culture that informed the debates around the foreign and the domestic, as well as the mediation between these two constructs, and hence the issue of translation in general.

A tension is tangible in Goethe's elaborations on the term in his conversation with Eckermann on 31 January 1827, in his comments on Carlyle's collection *German Romance* and other pronouncements from the same period. These comments introduce an opinion which was quite common in the nineteenth century that 'Deutschland ist die Wiege und Heimat der Weltliteratur' [Germany is the cradle and the home of world literature], that German culture, which had come into her own so relatively belatedly, formed the pinnacle and synthesis of world literary development and that fulfilling that role was the destiny of German culture.[3] Goethe's contemporary, Friedrich Schleiermacher, put it like this in his famous treatise *Über die verschiedenen Methoden des Übersetzens* [On the Different Methods of Translating, 1819]:

> And we must add to this [...] that our people, because of its esteem for the foreign and its own mediating nature, may be destined to unite all the jewels of foreign science and art together with our own in our own language, forming, as it were, a great historical whole that will be preserved at the centre and heart of Europe, so that now, with the help of our language, everyone will be able to enjoy all the things that the most different ages have given us as purely and perfectly as possible for one who is foreign to them.[4]

Much of this rather inflated sense of self-importance was based on the notion that the German language was particularly capable of recreating ancient Greek and Latin metres and that German was the true heir to the admired languages of European antiquity, and something of a conduit between the cradle of European culture and the national languages of the modern nation states. In spite of the importance of horizontal transfer and translation, in this light, the vertical one between ancient antiquity and contemporary languages remained the truly humanizing, educational task of any transfer effort: 'im Bedürfnis von etwas Musterhaften müssen wir immer zu den alten Griechen zurückgehen, in deren Werken stets der schöne Mensch dargestellt ist' [in our longing for something exemplary we always have to go back to the old Greeks in whose works there is always the presentation of beautiful man(kind).][5] For his own time, Goethe praises

3 Friedrich Engels, *Geschichte der Deutschen Literatur von den Anfängen bis zur Gegenwart* [1906], cited in Ulrich J. Beil, 'Die "verspätete Nation" und ihre Weltliteratur: Deutsche Kanonbildung im 19. und frühen 20. Jahrhundert', in *Kanon, Macht, Kultur: Theoretische, historische und soziale Aspekte ästhetischer Kanonbildungen*, ed. Renate von Heydebrand (Stuttgart: Metzler, 1998), 323–40 (p. 329).

4 Venuti (ed.), *The Translation Studies Reader*, 62.

5 Johann Peter Eckermann, *Gespräche mit Goethe in den letzten Jahren seines Lebens* (Berlin: Aufbau, 1984), 31 January 1827. Unless otherwise specified all translations into English in what follows are by F.K.

the new and more broadly based perspective on cultural achievement that crosslinguistic exchange permits:

> Es ist aber sehr artig, daß wir jetzt, bei dem engen Verkehr zwischen Franzosen, Engländern und Deutschen, in den Fall kommen, uns einander zu korrigieren. Das ist der große Nutzen, der bei einer Weltliteratur herauskommt und der sich immer mehr zeigen wird. (Eckermann, 15 July 1827)
> [It is quite pleasing that with the close exchange between the French, the English and the Germans nowadays, we have the opportunity to correct one another. That is the great advantage generated by world literature that will become increasingly apparent.]

Consequently, he advocates the engagement with foreign culture as a corrective against narrowminded national arrogance and a requirement for progress into the future. Following shortly after the period of the deepest divisions in Europe since the Thirty Years War, this stance takes on a hugely political meaning:

> Aber freilich, wenn wir Deutschen nicht aus dem engen Kreise unserer eigenen Umgebung herausblicken, so kommen wir gar zu leicht in diesen pedantischen Dünkel. Ich sehe mich daher gerne bei fremden Nationen um und rate jedem, es auch seinerseits zu tun. Nationalliteratur will jetzt nicht viel heißen, die Epoche der Weltliteratur ist an der Zeit, und jeder muß jetzt dazu wirken, diese Epoche zu beschleunigen. (Eckermann, 31 January 1827)
> [Indeed, if we Germans fail to look beyond the narrow circle of our own environment, we will easily deteriorate into a pedantic arrogance. That is why I like to look around, and I advise everybody to do the same for his part. National literature does not mean much nowadays, the epoch of world literature is of this time and everybody has to contribute to accelerate this epoch.]

In an era when the Revolutionary Wars, Napoleon's campaigns and the Wars of Liberation had just ravaged Europe, the 'epoch of world literature' is meant to heal rifts and to unite culturally what politically is thoroughly divided. The aim is mutual toleration:

> Eine wahrhaft allgemeine Duldung wird am sichersten erreicht, wenn man das Besondere der einzelnen Menschen und Völkerschaften auf sich beruhen läßt, bei der Überzeugung jedoch festhält, daß das wahrhaft Verdienstliche sich dadurch auszeichnet, daß es der ganzen Menschheit angehört. Zu einer solchen Vermittelung

> und wechselseitigen Anerkennung tragen die Deutschen seit langer Zeit schon bei. Wer die deutsche Sprache versteht und studiert, befindet sich auf dem Markte, wo alle Nationen ihre Waren anbieten; er spielt den Dolmetscher, indem er sich selbst bereichert.
> [A truly universal toleration can most certainly be achieved when one disregards the particularities of individual people and peoples while maintaining the conviction that whatever is truly meritorious is distinguished by belonging to all of humankind. The Germans have contributed to such a transfer and mutual acknowledgement for a long time. Whoever understands and studies the German language has entered the market place where all nations offer their wares; he plays the interpreter whilst enriching himself.][6]

Weltliteratur, in Goethe's explanation, is the cure to the divisions of Europe of the recent past, the true signature of the post-Napoleonic era. The aim of 'truly universal toleration' must be based on the acceptance of difference and on the affirmation of the shared values of humankind. Of course it constitutes a programme for post-war German cultural development that Goethe charges his countrymen with providing the forum (market place) and the service of *Dolmetscher* for this new era. Goethe's deliberations on translation in the wider context of healing rifts and preserving mutual values – here in its political significance naturally foregrounding contemporary horizontal translation – seem like a late application of the author's own poetic practice at the dawn of the classical era and then primarily enacted in the form of vertical translation of classical form and sentiment into the modern world in an attempt to exert a humanizing effect. His cycle *Römische Elegien* in particular constitutes an exercise in *Weltliteratur* avant la lettre. It is proof of the contention that German is the congenial vessel for the poetic treasures of Greek and Roman antiquity. It gives the impression of a harmonious blend between old and new, its aura is the cosmopolitan atmosphere of the very centre of the *oikoumene*, Rome itself. But it demonstrates one further dimension of Goethe's approach. The coinage of the term *Weltliteratur* seems to formulate on an idealistic, intercultural level a function also ascribed to literature on a concrete, personal level. Translation

6 Johann Wolfgang von Goethe, *Werke*. Hamburger Ausgabe, ed. Erich Trunz (Munich: Beck, 1981), vol. xii, 353.

is an act of appropriation and literary form is the receptacle of this process. Seen in this light, translation contributes to the aim of humanization, of tempering, soothing and harmonizing the uncouth, disparate and primeval. Any act of channelling and externalizing emotion, pouring emotion into an expressable form, must be considered as an act of translation.

The *Roman Elegies*

Written at a time when 'the poet was in a state of severe emotional unrest', Goethe's *Römische Elegien* is *the* cycle of poetry in the German language that celebrates the joy of physical love as spiritual fulfilment.[7] Yet it does so in a way that seems very controlled and restrained in its expressive and formal devices, if not its content. Written, as they were, in elegiac distichs, the elegies represent an attempt at a translation from the ancient to the modern in order to salvage, for Goethe's own time, the beauty and sentiment of the ancients. This is the central plank of the 'project aimed at the creation of a new, honest love poetry' that could, at the same time, serve the purpose of externalizing personal emotions.[8] In that vein, the cycle espouses a vision of human wholeness where physical love is but one avenue towards achieving contentment and completion, emotions that are not often discussed because they are seen as not controversial or exciting. Goethe's *Roman Elegies* form a testament to the author's connection, not only with his sexual partner, but also with the location in which the union took place, the symbol of European civilization, and thus with humankind in general. The cycle practices what the author himself, decades

7 David Barry, '"Sollte der herrliche Sohn uns an der Seite nicht stehn?": Priapus and Goethe's *Römische Elegien*', *Monatshefte* 82 (1990), 421–34 (423).

8 Hans Rudolf Vaget, 'Self-Censorship and Priapic Inspiration', in *A New History of German Literature*, ed. David Wellerby (Cambridge, Mass.: Harvard University Press, 2004), 424–8 (p. 427).

later, conceptualized as *Weltliteratur*, literature that transcends narrowly-defined notions of national literatures. Because of their erotic content, the *Roman Elegies* have experienced a very varied publication and translation history. The selections and decisions English translators have made achieve particular poignancy against the background of a reading of the cycle as celebrating connection, and thus as reuniting what had been severed, as engaging in an activity that the translator also defines as his own.[9] The translational act of adopting antique form and setting as a means of promoting the reconnection of something severed not only constituted an act of giving expression to certain emotions, but also moulded them into form and externalized something very personal and intimate.

Goethe's *Italian Journey* (so-called after his own travelogue – in reality it was a sojourn of some twenty-two months' duration) was Goethe's attempt to escape the feeling of disjointedness, alienation, stagnation in his private and professional life – a civilisatory condition. Frustrated with his duties as first minister of a tiny principality, unhappy with the impasse in his career as a writer, dissatisfied with his relationships, the *Italian Journey*, upon which he embarked secretly in September 1786, was in many ways a liberation, in other ways a new beginning and in some an initiation – an initiation into the realm of antiquity and the joys of fulfilled physical love. Written soon after his return from Italy, the *Roman Elegies* are the most important and most immediate literary fruit of this experience. At the same time they are also a reflection of his budding relationship with Christiane Vulpius back home, on which he embarked soon after his return and which was to last until her death in 1816. Virtually all critical evaluations of the *Roman Elegies* emphasize how the profound impact of his real Italian experiences – the relationship, first and foremost, with the Roman lady named once in the cycle as Faustina – is manifest in the celebratory tone of his verse. As Gert Ueding puts it regarding the appropriation of antiquity and the enjoyment of life's pleasures, artistic productivity and love, the experience of foreign culture and of the customs of a foreign

9 This aspect is further explored in Florian Krobb: 'Priapean Pursuits: Translation, World Literature and Goethe's *Roman Elegies*', *Orbis Litterarum* 65.1 (2010), 1–21.

people, in the *Roman Elegies* all of these these spheres are integrated into a whole, they belong together like art and love, nature and culture, undivided and unalienated.[10]

However, celebratory tone does not mean ecstatic, rapturous or tempestuous rhapsodizing, but the expression of elation in a measured, temperate way. Emotion in the content of the poems is channelled into, and conveyed by, the strictures of form of the chosen metre. Goethe's use of the genre designation 'Elegy' denotes not complaint or lament, but simply verse in distich form. This cycle is the first instance where the author consciously placed himself in an identifiable ancient poetic tradition. In this respect he engages in an act of vertical translation from an abstract antique model to contemporary German language and content, and he practices something approximating the ideal later espoused in the *Noten und Abhandlungen zum West-Östlichen Divan*. When he identifies here the ideal 'third epoch of translation' as the one that achieves 'perfect identity with the original, so that the one does not exist instead of the other but in the other's place', he has poetry in mind that replaces, supersedes the original, poetry that blends the old and the new.[11] In other respects the *Roman Elegies* also mark an artistic departure for Goethe: they are his first cycle of poems, connecting, as is the nature of such cycles, different themes into a coherent whole. Here the themes are love and antiquity, or better: Rome and its relics as the living site of antiquity, and the joyful physical relationship to the elusive Faustina.

The title Goethe eventually chose, *Römische Elegien*, and the original working title, *Erotica Romana*, express this thematic duality and the implicit translational act. These are love poems in a classical style, resurrecting the remote and abstract antique model for very contemporary, immediate and physically concrete expression. Amor is the symbol of the erotic content; Priapus, however, is the guide towards it, the patron of the undertaking since he populates the first and the last poem of the cycle, beginning and

10 Gerd Ueding, *Klassik und Romantik: Deutsche Literatur im Zeitalter der Französischen Revolution 1789–1815* (Munich: Hanser, 1987), 634–5.

11 Venuti (ed.), *The Translation Studies Reader*, 65.

end of the movement. Amor and Priapus are indistinguishable, they are the creators and the guarantors of the worldly wholeness, the pinnacle of fulfilment that, at least temporarily, enables the individual to transcend the Babelian rupture and to exclaim: 'O wie fühl' ich in Rom mich so froh!' [Oh, how happy I feel here in Rome!][12] The ecstasy expressed in such vociferation surely has a very emotive quality. In its simplicity (nine words of only one syllable each) this is meant to represent an outpouring of the most genuine, most heartfelt sentiment.

In Western culture, emotions are thought to be located primarily in an interior, private space, an imaginary spot that is defined in distinction to the physical condition of the human body and from its physical environment.[13] This interior sphere as the locus where emotions originate might be defined as soul or spirit or, utilizing a physical metaphor for an abstract concept, as heart. This conventional view is based on the assumption that any emotion has a pre-existence before it is expressed or made public in some shape or form. In this view, the expression of emotions is always a secondary act, a process of externalization and release into the environment governed by the restrictions of cultural convention and medium. The internal emotion, or so the assumption continues, will always be more genuine, more individual, more unadulterated than any expressed, published or displayed emotion could ever be, even if uttered with the utmost spareness like the motto-line 'O wie fühl' ich in Rom mich so froh!'. The internal emotion might also be considered as more joyful or painful, tender or extreme than the media of representation, the high arts of poetry, music, painting at one end of the scale, and gestures, mimics, physical action and formless speech at the other end, could ever permit. This is because the scope for the expression

12 Johann Wolfgang von Goethe, *Erotic Poems*, trans. David Luke. Introduction by Hans Rudolf Vaget (Oxford: Oxford University Press, 1997), 20–1 [first published 1988].

13 See Anne Fuchs and Sabine Strümper-Krobb, 'Einleitung: Lawrence Passmores I.D.K.-Problem oder die Leiblichkeit der Gefühle', in *Sentimente, Gefühle, Empfindungen: Zur Geschichte und Literatur des Affektiven von 1770 bis heute*, ed. by Anne Fuchs and Sabine Strümper-Krobb (Würzburg: Königshausen & Neumann, 2003), 17–26 (p. 18).

of emotions is conditioned by the limitations of the chosen medium, the necessity to give concrete form to something that is elusive and numinous, or so the argument goes. The concrete form of the expression is governed by social and cultural convention, by norms that censure the uncontrolled and unmanipulated exhibition of pure emotions.

Emotions, however, come in varieties that have an interpersonal dimension: they are triggered by other people, projected on to other people, exist primarily in relation to other people. Emotions, it could be argued, demand expression, otherwise they are pointless; only in their display do emotions actually come to life. Furthermore, the act of expression and externalization can serve as a kind of therapy, an act of transforming sentiments from an unconscious, diffuse and potentially destructive feeling into concrete, manageable entities, concepts even. As such, emotions can be imbued with purpose and direction, they can become productive. The process of moulding emotions into an expressive form, of shaping the display of feelings into something socially acceptable or interpersonally comprehensible, of communicating emotions through a given medium, can produce great art, can set free great energies. As a product of the necessity of finding a form for the expression of the profound transformative experience, Goethe's poems are testimony to the creative potential that the act of externalizing emotions releases. However, does the choice of a distinct and time-honoured form, the translational act of adopting an ancient form for contemporary and personal content, succeed in making the emotive core socially acceptable?

The dilemma was noted by contemporaries for whom the *Roman Elegies*, even in the curtailed form that suppressed some of the most explicit poems, namely the Priapean frame, seemed too private to be accepted within the norms of public standards of decency. It seemed particularly offensive that Goethe appeared to suggest a link between the poet's own personal experience and the erotic content of the poems, meaning that private emotions like longing and joy were made inappropriately public. As Johann Baptist von Alxinger put it in a letter to Karl August Böttiger on 25 March 1797:

> Propertius was able to say it out loud that he spent one happy night with a female friend. But what Herr von Goethe does before all of Germany in the *Horen* [the magazine in which the poems were originally published] with his mistress ... who would approve of that? What is annoying and offensive is not the thing itself, but the individuality, for here we see not a poet talking, but the Privy Councillor [Goethe's title of *Geheimer Rat*], the concrete person who does not seem to tell us a piece of fiction but a true story.[14]

The reference to Propertius highlights the view that public standards change, that artistic expressions not attributable to feelings of a living contemporary might be perceived as much more acceptable than those that incriminate an 'individual' of public standing in contemporary society. The contemporary readers' vindication of Propertius' erotic poetry as opposed to Goethe's also indicates that Goethe's strategy to use a very artificial and highly refined form as well as classical allusions and the evocation of an Italian atmosphere unfamiliar to his German public might not have garnered the desired effect. *Weltliteratur* (and with it the act of translation) fails when no agreement exists as to what the truly meritorious cultural core that belongs to all mankind actually is. Erotica, for Alxinger, should stay confined to Roman antiquity rather than be permitted to surface in provincial Weimar, just as emotions celebrating physical joys must remain interior, a private possession rather than a shared, externalized commodity.

The Priapean poems

The two Priapean poems which frame the *Roman Elegies* have the character of a prologue and an epilogue. These two poems belong to the stanzas that did not make it into the first publication of the cycle and consequently not into any other edition of Goethe's works until they appeared in a late supplementary volume of the magisterial *Weimarer Ausgabe* in 1914. An

14 Cited in Dieter Borchmeyer, *Die Weimarer Klassik: Eine Einführung* (Königstein im Taunus: Athenäum, 1980), 133–4.

English translation of the complete cycle of twenty-four, including the Priapean stanzas, only became available in 1988, namely in the authoritative bilingual edition based on the pioneering translation by David Luke.[15] The nineteenth-century editions in English only presented a small selection of elegies, if any at all, with a noticeable leaning towards poems with antique rather than erotic themes and poems containing general, non-concrete pronouncements on life and art and beauty. Preference is also given to poems with a solemn, even declamatory or sententious register such as Elegy I which, in the absence of the real prologue, had to assume the function of introduction and to establish the connection between the two themes of congenial locus and love:

> Saget, Steine, mir an, o sprecht, ihr hohen Paläste!
> Straßen, redet ein Wort! Genius, regst du dich nicht?
> [...]
> Eine Welt zwar bist du, o Rom; doch ohne Liebe
> Wäre die Welt nicht die Welt, wäre denn Rom auch nicht Rom.[16]

The ancient monuments are explicitly apostrophized as potential triggers of genuine experience and concomitant expression of emotion ('Genius' as Goethe puts it). The fusion of externalized emotion and congenial environment are, in this involuntary prologue, the two pillars upon which Goethe's poetry of channelled emotion rests. These lines were translated by Bowring in 1853 as if he wanted to surpass the sententious and declamatory character of the original:

> Speak, ye stones, I entreat! Oh speak, ye palaces lofty!
> Utter a word, oh ye streets! Wilt thou not, Genius, awake?
> [...] Thou art indeed a world, oh Rome; and yet, were Love absent,
> Then would the world be no world, then would e'en Rome be no Rome.[17]

15 Goethe, *Erotic Poems*.

16 Goethe, *Werke*, vol. i, 157.

17 Edgar Alfred Bowring, *The Poems of Goethe: translated in the original metres*, 2nd edn (London: George Bell & Sons, 1874), 291. *Goethe's Works*, vol. vii, Bohn's Standard Library 1st edn (London: John W. Parker & Son, 1853).

The grand gesture here overshadows the programmatic pronouncement. Newer translations avoid the heavy-handedness in their rendition of simple sentiments, personal realizations and appellations, a change that manifests itself not so much in a completely different vocabulary, but rather a simplified syntax: 'Speak to me stones, oh say, you lofty palaces, tell me …',[18] capturing more of the immediacy of the subject's interaction with the locus that facilitates the expression of emotions.

The elimination of the Priapean stanzas from all partial and more comprehensive renditions of the cycle in English during the nineteenth century is due to an act of delicate selectiveness or, to put it crudely, a prescriptive intervention and determination of what would be becoming for an English-speaking audience. [19] This is obviously due to moral sensitivities, the prologue ending, as it were, with an invocation of 'that red stake-shaft that sprouts from [Priapus'] loins', and the epilogue with the god's blessing to the author and his beloved: 'May your member not tire, until you have both […] finished the dance of your joy' (both lines in Luke's translation).[20] This seems to suggest that coarse eroticism prevails all the way in between. Far from it: not only are the emotions that guide the cycle far more subtle, far more delicate, far more nuanced than these two isolated extracts may suggest, the extracts themselves are far more sophisticated than at first sight they seem. The omission of the Priapean stanzas (and it is indeed only in these two poems that the offspring of Venus and anyone of three possible fathers, Bacchus, Adonis or Jupiter, makes an appearance) severs the connection to a strand of Latin poetry (the *Priapea*) that Goethe knew and deliberately emulated. Without them, the *Roman Elegies* constitute a general application of ancient form to modern personal sentiment, or a

18 Goethe, *Erotic Poems*, 5.

19 See Bowring's *The Poems of Goethe*. See also *Poems and Ballads of Goethe*, trans. W. Edmondstoune and Theodore Matrin (Edinburgh and London: William Plackwell & Sons, 1859); *The poems of Goethe, consisting of his Ballads and Songs and Miscellaneous Selections*, trans. by William Gibson (London: Simpkin Marshall & Co, 1883).

20 Goethe, *Erotic Poems*, 3 and 63.

rendition of a modern 'Roman' experience in the lofty, controlled, detached form of the Latin foil. With them, they constitute an actualization of a concrete, alas suppressed, thread of antique poetry, namely erotica.

The omission of the Priapean stanzas, intended to suppress the erotic content and symbolism, involuntarily affected another dimension of the imagery: that of Priapus as keeper of gardens whose 'weapon' fulfils the dual purpose of tending the plants and scaring off potential intruders, as explained in Benjamin Hederich's famous mythological handbook of the eighteenth century:

> Seine Sichel soll andeuten, entweder daß die Bäume und andere Gartengewächse immerzu beschnitten werden müssen, oder, daß er damit die Diebe [...] abhalten wolle.
> [His sickle is meant to indicate either that the trees and other garden plants have to be constantly pruned or that he wants to keep out the thieves with it.][21]

Significantly, this is exactly the function that Goethe attributes to Priapus in his prologue:

> Hier ist mein Garten bestellt, hier wart ich die Blumen der Liebe,
> Wie sie die Muse gewählt, weislich in Beete verteilt.
> Früchte bringenden Zweig, die goldenen Früchte des Lebens,
> Glücklich pflanzt ich sie an, warte mit Freuden sie nun.
> Stehe du hier an der Seite, Priap! ich habe von Dieben
> Nichts zu befürchten, und frei pflück und genieße wer mag.
> [Here my garden is growing, I tend here the flowers of love;
> They are the Muse's own choice, distributed wisely over different flower beds.
> Fruit-bearing branches, the golden fruits of life:
> Gladly I planted them, now I joyfully tend them.
> Stand beside them, Priap, I have nothing to fear from marauders;
> Anyone's welcome, it's all free to be picked and enjoyed.][22]

21 Benjamin Hederich, *Gründliches mythologisches Lexikon* (Leipzig: Gleditsch, 1770) [reprint Darmstadt: Wissenschaftliche Buchgesellschaft, 1996], 2084–5.

22 Goethe, *Erotic Poems*, 2–3.

Even though Goethe positions the fertility god demonstratively at the beginning of his cycle, he cheekily lets him occupy an unobtrusive spot 'an der Seite' ('at the side', not 'beside them' as Luke translates; there is no object in this clause). This is without question a pointer for readers to understand what follows. Furthermore, Priapus is reinterpreted as the guardian against hypocrites, not common thieves but 'verschämte Verbrecher', shamefaced miscreants, detractors whose crime *is* their shame. Preemptively Goethe excludes these people from the enjoyment of his poetry. By omitting the stanzas, the censors, who could surely recognize themselves in Goethe's description, excluded not only themselves but since they acted as translators or intermediaries, they sadly excluded others as well. Priapus' phallus is the stick with which to fend off those who harbour double standards, and thus the symbol of genuineness, of authenticity, of oneness and wholeness. The metaphorical garden, here denoting in the first instance the author's poetic undertaking and secondly also his setting – the beauty and splendour of the eternal city – obviously also evokes a state of innocence and purity. In this light, Priapus is the patron of the whole enterprise of poetic rectification of the civilisatory alienation of Goethe's life and, in the broader view, the patron of the translator's attempt to reconcile the ancient and the modern, the formal and the personal, the emotional and the sublime. Goethe's *Roman Elegies* use erotic symbolism with a view to transcending the realm of the merely erotic.

In the *Roman Elegies*, a plethora of conflicting tendencies are brought together and reconciled: past and present, culture and nature, the profane and the sacred, the personal and the universal, reason and intuition, learning and enjoyment, the high idealism of Winckelmannian views of antiquity and the popular, even coarse tradition of the Latin *Priapea*. This fusion and integration and balancing (pondering, comparing and seeing, too) is an act of translation in itself, translating the sensual into the artistic, the abstract into the experienced:

Oftmals hab ich auch schon in ihren Armen gedichtet
  Und des Hexameters Maß leise mit fingernder Hand
Ihr auf den Rücken gezählt.[23]
[Often I have composed my poetry in her embrace
  Counting the beats of the hexameter quietly with the fingers of my hand
Out on her back.][24]

The scene is of a truly erotic nature: two naked lovers in an embrace. And yet, the expression of their affection in terms of Greek metric patterns somehow tempers the eroticism, transcends it into a metaphor for something artistic and thus abstract. This blending of the harmony and symmetry epitomized by the Greek metre along with everything encapsulated by the Roman scene of intimacy epitomizes Goethe's vision of world literature in German. Here the ancient and the modern, the general and the personal, the world stage and the immensely intimate are fused. It also represents a channelling of emotions into form, a conversion of emotions that accompanies the translational act of externalization.

Erotic metaphor in the English translations

In their introductions and other commentary, the early English translators avoided any engagement with the content of the cycle. As if to divert attention from potentially offensive elements of the poems, they directed their interest, and that of their readers, to the poems' formal beauty, and this meant the perfection of the rhythmical language in the ancient metre. Even the translators' professions of modesty dwell on this very aspect: 'The beauties of the great original must inevitably be diminished, if not destroyed, in the process of passing through the translator's hands'.[25] The obsession with

23 Goethe, *Werke*, vol. i, 160.

24 Goethe, *Erotic Poems*, 14.

25 Edgar Alfred Bowring, 'The Translator's Original Dedication', in *The Poems of Goethe: translated in the original metres*, iii.

metric form, understandable though it might be from the practitioner's point of view, should not overshadow the interpreter's concern for content and substance. The ostensible beauty of an elevated register expressed in an appropriately archaic metre, and the interventions of contemporary translators regarding morally objectionable notions, exclude older translations from an investigation into the changes that occur in the process of translation. Thus a closer study of translational solutions to Goethe's technique of channelling emotions must dwell on more recent translations. Elegy VII (number IX in Luke's translation) starts with the evocation of the conditions which the Roman experience was instrumental in overcoming:

> O wie fühl' ich in Rom mich so froh! Gedenk' ich der Zeiten,
> Da mich graulicher Tag hinten im Norden umfing,
> Trübe der Himmel und schwer auf meine Scheitel sich senkte,
> Farb- und gestaltlos die Welt um den Ermatteten lag, ...
> [Oh, how happy I feel here in Rome, thinking of the days
> When, back in the North, grey days surrounded me,
> And dull heavens descended heavily upon my head,
> Colourless and formless the world lay around the wearisome ...]

Heaven here is a feature of the natural world, the site of clouds and the bringer of bad moods. The contrast to that situation, heralded with a forceful 'Nun', is established with reference to the 'Himmel's' metaphorical counterpart, 'Äther', which also introduces the theme of the speaker's quest for godlike existence in the guise of metaphors for healing and emotional contentment:

> Nun umleuchtet der Glanz des helleren Äthers die Stirne;
> Phöbus rufet, der Gott, Formen und Farben hervor.[26]
> [Now the shine of brighter ether lights my forehead;
> The sun-god conjures up forms and colours.][27]

These lines constitute a meta-reflection on Goethe's own activity. Translational externalization of internal sentiment can only ever be achieved

26 Goethe, *Werke*, vol. i, 162.
27 Goethe, *Erotic Poems*, 29.

through metaphor ('the shine of bright ether' on the 'forehead'). The result is formal and physically perceptible: 'forms [shapes] and colours'. While the forehead might be more associated with reason and thought, fire often serves to symbolize passionate feelings in that images of flames are a conventional device of finding expression for emotions. A triadic sequence organizes the movement in Elegy IX (XI in Luke). Starting with the image of fire, the two lovers' togetherness is portrayed as an ideal state: 'Und die erwärmete Nacht wird uns ein glänzendes Fest'. The image of ashes signifies an imperfect transitory state, but at the same time suggests the possibility of re-igniting the fire. The rekindling heat from the cooled-down remnants of the original source of the blissful state foreshadows renewal and reconnection. The beloved is cast as the agent of this renewal, in her character the promise of the third stage becomes visible:

> Morgen frühe geschäftig verläßt sie das Lager der Liebe,
> Weckt aus der Asche behend Flammen aufs neue hervor.
> Denn vor andern verlieh der Schmeichlerin Amor die Gabe,
> Freude zu wecken, die kaum still wie zu Asche versank.[28]

Uncharacteristically for the refined stylist Goethe, the repeated use of the verb 'wecken' indicates that the imperfect stage is one that already contains, however dormant, the promise of the third, just as the ashes preserve the embers for later re-ignition. The appellation of the beloved as 'Schmeichlerin', in this light, carries the meaning of coaxing the dormant energies back to existence. The woman is attributed agency in achieving the new state. The two final couplets of the poem, as cited, are quite different in character. In the first distich, the adjectives 'geschäftig' and 'behend' convey the image of adroit domesticity, they denote traditional traits of the homemaker. The register of the last couplet is quite elevated in contrast. The reference to the divine as having bestowed upon her the 'Gabe' (gift as opposed to present), the words 'Schmeichlerin' and 'verleihen' as well as the preceding genitive, all contribute to the impression of elevated register and solemn sentiment. In his English translation of 1974

28 Goethe, *Werke*, vol. i, 163.

Lind maintains the repetition of the verb and interprets 'Schmeichlerin' as coaxer; he relates it, however, to the first person voice of the story – she coaxes not him but the flames – and adds 'to warm us again', thus shifting the focus from the action to the beneficiaries. He also severs the link to the divine by translating Amor as Love and interpreting the gift as a talent. The terms 'bustle away' and 'love-nest', though, strike the right tone of the domestic, cosy distich; yet the register shift is not quite pronounced in the final couplet:

> Early next morning she'll bustle away from our love nest,
> To wake the flames from their ashes to warm us again.
> For Love gave my coaxer the talent above any other
> To waken a joy that has scarcely grown still as the ash.[29]

Luke also substitutes Love for Amor and inserts a possessive pronoun that removes the sense of abstract agency on the Schmeichlerin's part, defining the result of the re-ignition as 'pleasure', suggesting physical reward, in place of the term 'Freude' or joy which can carry a theological meaning. The aspect of waking and the concomitant implication of dormancy is lost altogether:

> Early tomorrow she'll busily rise from the bed of our loving;
> Quickly the ashes she'll stir, soon the bright flames she'll renew.
> For this especial gift Love gave to my dearest of charmers:
> Pleasure no sooner burns low than she can wake it again.[30]

Cheesman, finally, has a doubling of the verb, but the notion of stirring deviates from the source text and it rather undermines the broadness of the movements, directed towards outside the ashes; and the fillers 'instantly' and 'just', as well as using 'still' as a predicate rather than an adverb confuse relations and suggest commotion where the source text exudes tranquillity. In addition his version seems to carry some more sexual innuendo than

29 Johann Wolfgang Goethe, *Roman Elegies and Venetian Epigrams: A Bilingual Text*, trans. and ed. L.R. Lind (Lawrence: The University of Kansas Press, 1974), 51.

30 Goethe, *Erotic Poems*, 25.

both other attempts, but the centre of that is the first of the two distichs rather than, as in the source text, the second:

> Early next morning she wakes up again, and leaving the love-bed she
> Stirs the ashes, so flame instantly rises again.
> Amor's favourite, specially, flatterer, gifted with stirring
> Joy awake when it's just settled like ash, and is still.[31]

The more conventional, but easily accessible phrase 'to stir the ashes' with its direct object, that two of the translators opt for, shifts the image from a directional movement of creation and emergence to an internal, circular movement. These observations illustrate how translators, led by the requirements of the target language, the strictures of their chosen rhythm and the necessity to clarify, arrive at solutions that might not necessarily conform with certain interpretative approaches. Translation is interpretation, but translation is also always based on interpretation, the translator's reading of the source text. And thirdly, translation analysis must be based on interpretation too, since the criteria for evaluation are derived by the analyst from his or her reading of the text. Applying my criteria, I have come to the conclusion that the translations of Goethe's *Roman Elegies* studied here miss the point, if they don't suppress the poignant verses altogether. But, to be sure, they only miss *my* interpretative point. Their own points they make firmly and persuasively.

One dimension of Goethe's Roman experience was indeed erotic. But the erotic playfulness is a means to an end, not an end in itself. It is the metaphor in which the restored completeness expresses itself. It is a fundamentally theological, yet also fundamentally secularized world view for which the fusion of physical love and classical beauty provides the vessel. Priapus is the mentor of refined emotions and the guide to a secularized vision of healing, containing and converting emotions. He is the steward in Goethe's first true practice of *Weltliteratur*. But he is also the figure that shows up the limitations regarding the flight of this piece of *Weltliteratur* into the world by means of translation.

31 Johann Wolfgang Goethe, 'Roman Elegies 1790', trans. Tom Cheesman, *Writing Ulster* 1 (1990–91), 138–41 (139).

MICHAEL CLARKE

Translation and Transformation: A Case Study from Medieval Irish and English

Traditionally we were taught that the translator is the betrayer of his source text, or at best a passive intermediary who allows the reader to forget that he exists. In our time it has been a source of new vigour to realize that that view was grimly reductive, and we can now see the translator as a powerful agent whose authority is all the more deeply embedded when it is unacknowledged.[1] The urgency of this insight is borne out especially clearly by the pivotal role of the professional interpreter in arenas where political and linguistic worlds collide, like the interrogation rooms of Guantánamo Bay or in the multilingual creativity of modern life.[2] But the principle applies just as much when a literary translator takes a text from one cultural context and recreates it in another. Poised between two systems of thought and communication, he acts as gatekeeper between them and determines their relative status in terms of power and dominance. Implicitly, also, he poses the Whorfian question: to what extent are meanings and cultural structures separable from the forms of the particular language in which they were first expressed?[3] I want to use this perspective as the starting-point for investigating an extraordinary episode in the history of translation: the creative project that was carried out under parallel forms in medieval

1 See Lawrence Venuti, *The Translator's Invisibility: a History of Translation* (London: Routledge, 1995) and *The Scandals of Translation: Towards an Ethics of Difference* (London: Routledge, 1998).

2 See Cormac Ó Cuilleanáin and Michael Cronin's articles in this volume.

3 Dedre Gentner and Susan Goldin-Meadow, eds, *Language in Mind: Advances in the Study of Language and Thought* (Cambridge, Mass.: MIT Press, 2003).

England and Ireland, when the vernacular languages were the vehicles for a startlingly bold form of translation practised by sophisticated *literati*[4] steeped in international monastic learning.[5]

The global context in Insular self-representation

Because the medieval literatures of these islands have so often been treated as gateways to ethnic prehistories (English and Germanic, Irish and Celtic as the case may be) it is easy to forget that their creators' sense of identity was conditioned by their remoteness from the heartlands of European and Christian identity. Britain and Ireland lay on the edge of a world centred on Rome or Jerusalem, and Irish and Old English are the languages of peoples who never formed part of the Roman empire. Hence, for example, the cosmopolitan Irishman Columbanus takes it as a measure of the power of the Church that its message reached 'as far as the western regions of earth's furthest strand, over the surge of the channels, over the dolphins' backs ...

4 The term *literati* is now conventional, especially among scholars working on the Irish evidence, to gloss over our continuing uncertainty about the social and cultural horizons of the authors of our texts. See Michael Richter, 'The personnel of learning in early medieval Ireland' in *Irland und Europa im frühen Mittelalter*, ed. Proinséas Ní Chatháin and Michael Richter (Stuttgart: Klett-Cotta, 1996), 275–308; and Thomas Charles-Edwards, *Early Christian Ireland* (Cambridge: Cambridge University Press, 2000), 264–81.

5 English and Irish monastic culture have almost always been studied separately, and synthetic treatments are rare. Useful surveys are Andy Orchard, 'Latin and the vernacular languages: the creation of a bilingual textual culture', in *After Rome*, ed. Thomas Charles-Edwards (Oxford: Oxford University Press, 2003), 191–220 for the earlier part of the period discussed in this chapter; Dáibhí Ó Cróinín, 'Writing', in *From the Vikings to the Normans*, ed. Wendy Davies (Oxford: Oxford University Press, 2003), 169–202, for the later part.

even to us'.[6] Likewise the Northumbrian scholar Bede constructs his grand narrative of Christianity in Britain around a struggle between those who sought conformity with Rome and those who persisted in deviating from the norms laid down there.[7] Puzzling though it may seem to us, Bede even bases his geographical description of his native land on the account written three hundred years beforehand by a follower of St Augustine, Orosius – a man who had presumably never set foot in Britain himself.[8] Even more strangely, elements of the national origin-myth developed by the medieval Irish were based on reinterpreted or 'disunderstood' stray verbal collocations from Orosius' universal *History Against the Pagans* and lore from another work of remote Continental origin, the encyclopaedic *Etymologies* of Isidore of Seville.[9]

In the context of this sense of remoteness, one of the chief intellectual projects of the Insular *literati* was to invent or renegotiate the relationship between their own races and the Mediterranean centre. The origin legend of the British took them back to the Roman origins and exiled wanderings of a grandson of Aeneas of Troy, the eponymous founder-hero Britus or Brutus,[10] while the Irish *Lebor Gabála* traces the origins of the Gaels

6 Columbanus, *Letter* 5.11, trans. G.S.M. Walker, *Sancti Columbani Opera* (Dublin: Dublin Institute for Advanced Studies, 1997).

7 On the intellectual horizons of the *Historia Ecclesiastica* see esp. Patrick Wormald, *The Times of Bede: Studies in Early English Christian Society and its Historian* (Oxford: Blackwell, 2006).

8 See Natalia Lozovsky, '*The Earth is our Book*': *Geographical Knowledge in the Latin West ca. 400–1000* (Ann Arbor: University of Michigan Press, 2000), 87–8.

9 On the 'tower of Breogan' based on the Spanish city-name Brigantia, and the 'Spanish soldier', *miles Hispaniae* becoming Míl of Spain, see Dáibhí Ó Cróinín, 'Ireland, 400–800', in *A New History of Ireland Vol. 1: Prehistoric and Early Ireland*, ed. Dáibhí Ó Cróinín (Oxford: Oxford University Press, 2003), 185–6, citing Mac Néill's observations of 1921. This line of interpretation goes back even further, to an extraordinary note by Todd in his edition of the Irish Nennius: James Henthorn Todd, ed. and trans., *The Irish Version of the Historia Brittonum of Nennius* (Dublin: Irish Archaeological Society, 1848), 238, note 'n'. See also Rolf Baumgarten, 'The geographical orientation of Ireland in Isidore and Orosius', *Peritia* 3 (1984), 189–203.

10 See Nennius, *Historia Brittonum* ch. 10.

back to Scythia, from where they travel via Egypt, Mesopotamia and the Mediterranean to Spain and along the Ocean to Ireland.[11] Likewise the Irish annalists and the poets set up precise correspondences in timing between events in Irish and continental history and pseudohistory: and these synchronisms often resonate thematically, as when they assign the mythic battle of Moytura to the same point in time as the sack of Troy,[12] or when the wars and deaths of the heroes of Ulster are intertwined with the events of the Gospels.[13] In the case of Irish (though apparently not English), even the language has an origin legend of its own. In the *Lebor Gabála*, the ancestor Fénius Farsaid refuses to join in building the tower of Babel and is rewarded when God allows him to choose 'what is best out of every language', the result being Irish.[14] This particular story may seem wry and folksy, but it has a counterpart in the practical and scientific juxtaposition of languages carried out in the early glossaries, where vernacular words are etymologized from supposed parallels in Latin, Greek and Hebrew. As we will see, this preoccupation with parallelism finds a narrative expression 'writ large' in the highly sophisticated strategies of translation that were applied to the canonical literature of the eastern Mediterranean heartlands, both Biblical history and pagan heroic narrative.

11 See John Carey and John T. Koch, *The Celtic Heroic Age*, 4th edn (Aberystwyth: Celtic Studies Publications, 2003), 226–71, with Kim McCone, *Pagan Past and Christian Present in Early Irish Literature* (Maynooth: An Sagart, 1991).

12 See Peter Smith, ed. and trans., *Three Historical Poems Ascribed to Gilla Cóemáin: a Critical Edition of the Work of an Eleventh-Century Irish Scholar* (Münster: Nodus Publikationen, 2007), 238.

13 John V. Kelleher, 'The Táin and the Annals', *Ériu* 22 (1971) 107–27.

14 See Carey and Koch, *The Celtic Heroic Age*, 229–30, and for the variant version in the grammatical tract *Auraicept na n-Éces* see Anders Ahlqvist, ed. and trans., *The Early Irish Linguist: an Edition of the Canonical Part of the Auraicept na n-Éces* (Helsinki: Societas Scientiarum Fennica, 1983), 48. Useful discussion by Paul Russell, '"What was best of every language": the early history of the Irish language', in *New History of Ireland Vol. 1: Prehistoric and Early Ireland* ed. Dáibhí Ó Cróinín (Oxford: Oxford University Press, 2003), 405–7.

Cross-cultural translation in the Old English Biblical poems

I begin with the Old English poems that render books of the Old Testament into vernacular alliterative verse.[15] The bulk of these poems (*Genesis*, *Exodus*, and *Daniel*) are preserved as a series in the manuscript known as Junius 11, while a further example, *Judith*, is found in the Nowell Codex which also preserves *Beowulf*.[16] The origins of this technique of Biblical translation seem to go back to continental Germanic poetry of the Carolingian period, and there are cognate English and Carolingian versions of a founder hero – the herdsman who is inspired by God in a dream to begin composing Biblical narratives in the traditional mode and language of vernacular pagan song.[17] The surviving poems expand and recast the Biblical narratives on a grand scale, and it is obvious that they were never intended as faithful renderings subservient to the word-for-word sense of the originals. Rather, the poems reflect a strategy of 'analogical imitation', in Doane's neat phrase,[18] and their achievement is to absorb the source material into

15 See in general Paul G. Remley, *Old English Biblical Verse* (Cambridge: Cambridge University Press, 1996) and Malcolm R. Godden, 'Biblical poetry: the Old Testament', in *The Cambridge Companion to Old English Literature*, edited by Godden and Michael Lapidge (Cambridge: Cambridge University Press, 1991), 206–26. Beyond the scope of this essay are the verse renderings of the Psalms in the Paris Psalter, which are more closely akin to word-for-word translation than are the poems discussed here.

16 It remains unclear whether there was ever a thematic reason for the inclusion of *Beowulf* and *Judith* together in the Nowell Codex. Orchard argues that *Judith* can be seen as paralleling *Beowulf* as a narrative of 'the fatal humiliation of overweening pride' (*Pride and Prodigies: Studies in the Monsters of the* Beowulf-*Manuscript* (Cambridge: D.S. Brewer, 1995)) 3–12, at p. 5); but it is harder to relate *Judith* to the compiler's evident interest in the monstrous – unless that concern drew him either to Holofernes' grotesque behaviour or Judith's anomalous assumption of heroic behaviours unsuited to a woman.

17 See Bede, *Ecclesiastical History* 4.24, with A.N. Doane (ed.), *The Saxon Genesis*. (Madison, Wisconsin: University of Wisconsin Press, 1991), 3–8.

18 A.N. Doane (ed.), *Genesis A* (Madison, Wisconsin: University of Wisconsin Press, 1978), 49.

the vernacular poetic tradition – in effect, to 'nativize' the learned foreign Latinity of the Bible. The narratives of sacred history become as authentically embedded in the adoptive language as are poems set in the past of the Northern world, like *Beowulf* itself.

There is evidence that this practice was subtle and strategic. *Judith*, for example, not only enacts a moral message but explores the ideology of heroism by applying traditionally masculine values to a female protagonist,[19] and *Exodus* hints at an allegorical interpretation in which the journey of the Israelites is an image of the journey of the human soul.[20] But the most striking example is in the *Genesis* poem. There, Satan's sin of pride is called by the name of *ofermede*, meaning an excess of mental spirit and energy, *mod*:

> Þa hit se allwalda   eall gehyrde
> þæt his engel ongan   ofermede micel
> ahebban wið his hearran ... (*Genesis B* 293–4)
> [Then the All-Ruler heard everything, that his angel had begun to take up great 'over-spirit' against his lord ...]

The term chimes with the value-system of contemporary heroic ideology, and the usage here strikingly recalls the famous attribution of *ofermod*, 'excessive valour', to Byrhtnoth, the hero whose reckless risk-taking exposes himself and his people to destruction in *The Battle of Maldon* (89).[21] Compare the terms in which Satan's example persuades other rebel angels to follow:

19 Mark Griffith, ed., *Judith* (Exeter: Exeter University Press, 1997), 62–93.

20 See Godden, 'Biblical poetry: the Old Testament', 217–19; Peter J. Lucas, ed., *Exodus*, 2nd edn (Exeter: Exeter University Press, 1994), 45–51, 61–9.

21 For *ofermod* applied to Satan see also *Solomon and Saturn II* 273 in Daniel Anlezark (ed. and trans.), *The Old English Dialogues of Solomon and Saturn* (Cambridge: Boydell and Brewer, 2007), 92. On the much-debated problems of *ofermod* in *The Battle of Maldon* see esp. Helmut Gneuss, '*The Battle of Maldon* 89: Byrhtnoth's *ofermod* again', *Studies in Philology* 73 (1976) 117–37; Fred C. Robinson, 'God, death and loyalty in the *Battle of Maldon*' [originally published 1979], in *Old English Literaturei*, ed. R.M. Liuzza (New Haven: Yale University Press, 2002), 425–44;

... hie hyra gal beswac,
engles oferhygd ... (*Genesis B* 327–8)
[Their folly beguiled them, the 'over-valour' of the angel.]

Here *oferhygd*,[22] virtually synonymous with *ofermod*, makes Satan's sin into the same error as might await a contemporary prince who has risen too far upward. In Beowulf's hour of triumph, the older king Hrothgar warns him that if the energy of the successful warrior turns to tyrannical selfishness, it will bring about his ruin when *oferhygda dæl*, his 'portion of pride', rises and swells within him (*Beowulf* 1740).

A.M. Doane has argued forcefully that the *Genesis* poem represents Satan's rebellion in terms of the tensions inherent in Germanic warrior society. Assuming that the discourse in the surviving text goes back to the earlier Carolingian version (of which the corresponding section is lost),[23] Doane sees God as the representative of a modernizing social hierarchy, Satan as a throwback to the social structures of an earlier age:

> Satan is represented as wanting to replace the hierarchical system of governance by vassalage, what would have seemed natural and 'modern' to the ninth-century Carolingian poet and his audience, with the older idea of the 'free' comitatus ... In the older system, from the point of the view of the *dryhten* [lord], there are no upward-looking hierarchies, only downward-linking bonds depending on personal and shifting loyalties ... Satan is, in fact, a picture of just such a petty lord in rebellion; in particular he would have fit among the contemporary Saxons, who traditionally recognised no king and whose aristocrats with their pretensions of independence perennially plagued the Carolingians. (Doane, *The Saxon Genesis* p. 123)

John D. Niles, 'Maldon and mythopoesis' [originally published 1994], also in *Old English Literature*, pp. 445–74.

22 Again applied to Satan in the related poem *Christ and Satan*, 50.

23 This is not the place to discuss the relationship between the two parts into which *Genesis* is conventionally divided – *Genesis B* for the section demonstrably based on an Old Saxon orginal, *Genesis A* for that which seems to be directly composed in English. Since the two are presented in Junius 11 as a single continuous text without subdivisions, it will be sufficient here to treat them as the unity that they evidently constituted for the compilers of the manuscript.

If this is right, the dynamic of transference runs deeper than the level of language and style: the effect of the poem is to reconstruct *Genesis* not only in the literary world of the target language but also in its cultural and ideological structures.

Following Doane, it is tempting to associate this with the rhetorical strategies that were brought into play when the Germanic peoples were being converted to Christianity; but of course this applies only to the earlier, Continental phase in the poem's development. A question mark still hangs over the interpretation of the poem in its contemporary Anglo-Saxon context, since the considerations that Doane invokes would have been incidental at best in the thoroughly Christianized world of tenth-century England. Working towards an answer, I suggest that it would be a mistake to see the project entirely in didactic or exegetical terms. As a further example,[24] consider a passage from the Latin text of *Genesis*:[25]

> Numeravit expeditos vernaculos suos trecentos decem et octo et persecutus est eos usque Dan. Et divisis sociis inruit super eos nocte percussitque eos ... (*Genesis 14* 14–15)
> [[Abraham] led forth his trained men, born in his house, three hundred and eighteen, and pursued as far as Dan. And he divided himself against them by night, he and his servants, and smote them ...]

In the poem this is recreated as follows:

> þa se halga heht his heorðæwerod
> wæpna onfon. he thær wigena fand,
> æscberendra, eahtatyne
> and þreohund eac þeodenholdra
> þara þe he wiste þæt meahte wel æghwylc
> on fyrd wegan fealwe linde.
> Him þa Abraham gewat and þa eorlas þry

24 See Andy Orchard, 'Conspicuous heroism: Abraham, Prudentius, and the Old English *Genesis*', in R.M. Liuzza (ed.), *The Poems of Junius 11: Basic Readings* (London: Routledge, 2002), 119–36.

25 I quote for convenience from the Vulgate, with the proviso that the text used by the poet will equally likely have been in the *Vetus Latina* tradition.

þe him ær treowe sealdon mid heora folce getrume ...
Rincas wæron rofe, randas waegon
forð fromlice on foldwege.
hildewulfas herewicum neh
gefaron hæfdon ... (*Genesis A* 2039–52)

[Then the holy one commanded his hearth-company to take up weapons. He found there eighteen and three hundred of warriors, ash-spearbearers, lord-trusty men, and he knew that each one of them would bring his tawny linden-shield to the troop. With them Abraham went forth, and the three earls that before had pledged their troth to him, and a company of their folk ... The warriors were eager, they bore their shields forth boldly from the earth-way. The battle-wolves came near to the army-camp ...]

Does the elaboration of the battle-sequence contribute anything to the meaning of the story in terms of theology or sacred history? Not that I can see: indeed, it is disturbing to see Abraham's men named as 'battle-wolves', a name that seems ideologically loaded in a negative way when applied to pagan Vikings in *The Battle of Maldon* (*wælwulfas*, *Maldon* 96).[26] But there is no need to hear a jarring note here if we see the effect in terms of poetic ownership rather than didactic meaning: the point is that the Germanic heroic colouring draws Abraham fully and recognisably into the world-picture and poetic traditions of the English. It is significant that Junius 11 is a large decorated codex evidently intended for display in a church, as if it were to be encountered as a precious artifact in an ecclesiastical setting – declaring by its presence that the Christian perspective on history and morality has become part of this remote northern world and its barbarous tongue.

The audacity of the Old Testament poems is striking by contrast with the conventional prose translations of sacred texts into Old English – notably Aelfric's version of the first six books of the Bible, and the anonymous Old English Gospels. Here the characteristic pattern is an explicit concern

26 See Niles, 'Maldon and mythopoesis', and note the similar *heorawulfas* applied more comfortably to the Egyptians at *Exodus* 191.

for accuracy and simplicity.[27] These latter translations were almost certainly intended to help students or priests with imperfect knowledge of Latin, and they follow the phraseology of the originals so closely that they are only a step removed from 'gloss-translations', the accumulated piecemeal notes of vernacular equivalents that were added to Bibles to aid readers in translation at sight. The contrast with the poems could not be greater in terms of the hierarchical relationship between the two languages: where the poems show target language overpowering source, the gloss-translation allows the target language only a subservient role, most obviously when it is physically fragmented on the page of the manuscript.[28]

Biblical lore transformed in Irish: *Saltair na Rann* and Blathmac

Turning now to the evidence from Ireland, the corpus is rich in examples of cross-cultural reinvention. Closest in kind to the Old English poems is the extraordinary poetic sequence *Saltair na Rann*, which includes a long sequence of renderings of key Bible stories into Irish verse of the kind known as *deibide*.[29] Not all of *Saltair na Rann* can be matched to specific

27 Robert Stanton, *The Culture of Translation in Anglo-Saxon England* (Cambridge: D.S. Brewer, 2002) ch.1 and *passim*. The principles of accurate translation are explicitly discussed in the Preface to King Alfred's translation of Gregory's *Pastoral Care*: see Malcolm R. Godden, 'Literary language' in R.M. Hogg (ed.), *The Cambridge History of the English Language Volume 1: The Beginnings to 1066*, 490–534 (Cambridge: Cambridge University Press, 1991), 514–15.

28 See Suzanne Reynolds, *Medieval Reading: Grammar, Rhetoric and the Classical Text* (Cambridge: Cambridge University Press, 1996).

29 The principal modern publication of *Saltair na Rann* is David Greene and Fergus Kelly, *The Irish Adam and Eve Story from Saltair na Rann: Vol. 1: Text and Translation* (Dublin: Dublin Institute for Advanced Studies, 1976), with Murdoch's commentary referenced below. John Carey's important articles on the earlier, cosmological sections are beyond the scope of this essay: see John Carey, *King of Mysteries: Early*

source texts, but the well-known section on the story of Adam and Eve is derived from a known Latin original, the apocryphal *Life of Adam and Eve*.[30] Just as in the English poems, the translation is a thorough transformation into the aesthetic and poetic standards of the target language. I cite a fine example from the account of Adam's toils after his exile from Eden, when he wanders the world and finds that there is no better food to eat than the lowly vegetation of the earth:

> Ro-la Adam cúaird co léir
> hi focus, hi n-etercéin,
> ni fuair ni do biud bad glan
> fo diud acht lubai in talman.
>
> 'Lubai in talman, glas a ndath,
> bíad na n-anman n-indligthech,
> nidad tlaithi dun fri feis
> iar mbíadaib blaithi Parduis.' (1565–72)
>
> [Adam made a circuit diligently, near and far; he finally found no pure food but the herbs of the earth. 'The herbs of the earth, green in colour, the food of the brute animals, they are not easy for us to eat after the mild foods of Paradise'.] (tr. Greene and Kelly)

To see how thoroughly this has been 'nativized', we find a close comparison in the famous poems of *Buile Shuibhne*,[31] where the king is cursed and exiled, wanders over the land in the likeness of a bird and has to live on herbs and cresses:

Irish Religious Writings (Dublin: Four Courts Press, 2000), 97–124, and the references there.

30 Brian Murdoch, *The Irish Adam and Eve Story from Saltair na Rann, Vol. 2: Commentary* (Dublin: Dublin Institute for Advanced Studies, 1976); also Murdoch, *The Apocryphal Adam and Eve in Medieval Europe* (Oxford: Oxford University Press 2009), ch.5.

31 J.G. O'Keeffe (ed. and tr.), *Buile Shuibhne/ The Adventures of Suibhne Geilt* (London: Irish Texts Society, 1910).

Dúairc an bhetha bheith gan teach,
as truagh an bhetha, a Chríosd chain,
sásadh biorair bairrghlais búain,
deogh uisge fhúair a glais ghlain.

Feis oidhche gan chluimh a ccoill
i mullach croinn dosaigh dhlúith,
gan coisteacht re guth ná glór,
a mhic Dé, is mór an mhúich. (§61)

[Wretched is the life of one homeless,
sad is the life, O fair Christ!
a meal of fresh green-tufted watercress,
a drink of cold water from a clear stream.

Sleeping of nights without covering in a wood
in the top of a thick, bushy tree,
without hearing voice or speech;
O son of God, great is the misery!] (tr. O'Keeffe)

The conceptual triangle of exile, loneliness and the eating of lowly herbs informs both images, and they participate in a single poetic world-picture. *Buile Shuibhne* in its present form dates from perhaps two centuries after *Saltair na Rann*, but it would be unnecessarily mechanical to see the former passage as an imitation or adaptation of the latter, still more to regard this image in *Saltair na Rann* as an imitation of a putative early version of the *Buile Shuibhne* poems. Rather, they bear witness to a single dynamic of cultural absorption: this is how *Genesis* sounds when transmuted by a Gaelic voice, and equally the suffering of Suibhne takes on a new theological seriousness through the parallel.

But we must ask again: how deep is this transformation? With *Saltair na Rann* it is often hard to tell in a particular instance whether we are faced with a purely linguistic equivalence or a more profound, even argumentative mapping. For example, when *Saltair na Rann* tells the story of the contest between Moses and the Egyptian priests it calls the latter *druid*, 'druids' (l. 3849); is this simply a mechanical translation of Latin *magus*, or does it reflect some scholar-poet's desire to identify parallels between the pagan past of Ireland and that of the ancient Mediterranean?[32] The question cannot be answered, and perhaps the answer would have been different for two listeners or readers even when the poem was first composed. Occasionally, however, a group of concepts is translated systematically into an Irish cultural framework, as if the poet is deliberately working towards a sense of equivalence between two far-flung worlds.[33] There is a neat example in the account of Adam's attempt to atone for his sin after his expulsion from Eden. According to the original Latin *Life of Adam and Eve*, Adam fasts in the river Jordan for forty days and nights to demonstrate his penitence. In the Irish version, however, the procedure is more complex:

> Ro gaid Adam, hitgi thren,
> iarum for sruth n-Iordanen,
> co troisced lais for Dia ndil
> co huilib hilmilaib. (1629–32)
> [Adam then prayed, a strong request, the river Jordan, that it, with all its many animals, should fast with him against dear God.]

The key word here is *troisced*, subjunctive from *troscaid*, 'he fasts'. The corresponding verbal noun *troscud*, 'fasting' or 'hunger-strike', names a custom peculiar to early Irish law: a client could try to force his lord to acknowledge his plea by starving himself on his doorstep.[34] Adam's fasting is conceptualized in this way as a hunger-strike *against* God, *for Dia*. The poet has evidently started from the words *ieiunans ... ante conspectum Dei*, 'fasting before the sight of God' in the source text, and has reconfigured the image so that it enacts the Irish legal procedure. In the law of *troscud* the complainant's retainers could join him in his hunger-strike to increase

32 See McCone, *Pagan Past and Christian Present in Early Irish Literature*, 33–4.

33 The discussion of cultural translation that I present here bears comparison with the acute discussion of the Saul and David section of the poem recently published online by Laurence Hunt (http://www.focalfactory.eu/solasanlae/snar/index113–117.htm).

34 Fergus Kelly, *A Guide to Early Irish Law* (Dublin: Dublin Institute for Advanced Studies, 1988), 182–3; Murdoch, *The Irish Adam and Eve Story*, 112.

the pressure, and in *Saltair na Rann* the animals and the river itself play this part beside Adam:

Ro gādatar dib-līnaib
Adam is sruth, hilmīlaib;
trúag ro fhersat a nnúal n-án
fri slúag n-úag na noí noebgrād. (1641–4)
[They both prayed, Adam and the stream with many creatures; pitifully they poured out their noble lamentation to the pure host of the nine holy orders.]

Here if anywhere we see a radical and systematic strategy, exploring correspondences and divergences between the social ideologies of Irish and Biblical worlds.

Mappings of this kind seem to have been part of a more widespread project in early Irish monastic literature. There is a neat example in the devotional poems of Blathmac,[35] a collection stemming from the mysterious spiritual milieu of the Céli Dé in the eighth century.[36] Blathmac speaks of the Jews' murder of Christ in the following terms:

Ainbli gnúisi, condai fir
Ro-fersat in fingail-sin;
Céin ba diïb a máthair
Ba diäll for fírbráthair ...

Cach feb tecomnacht in rí
Do Iudib ara célsini,
Batar moíni do mogaib;
Ro-coillset a cobfolaid. (§103, 106)

[Of shameless countenance and wolflike were the men who perpetrated that kinslaying; since his mother was of them it was treachery towards a true kinsman ... Every advantage that the King had bestowed on the Jews in return for their clientship was

35 James Carney (ed. and tr.), *The Poems of Blathmac* (London: Irish Texts Society, 1964).
36 Westley Follett, *Céli Dé in Ireland* (Cambridge: Boydell and Brewer, 2006), 168–70.

'wealth to slaves' [i.e. gifts wasted on the unworthy]; they violated their counter-obligations.] (tr. Carney, adapted)

As James Carney showed,[37] Blathmac sees the relationship between God or Christ and the devotee in terms of an Irish social institution based on the bonds of reciprocity. Here, the crime of the Jews is conceptualized in terms of the mutual obligations of kinship on the one hand and the master-follower relationship on the other. Because Jesus' mother was a Jew, they were guilty of kinslaying (*fingal*); because his father was God and the Hebrews were bound to God by a relationship of loyalty as client followers (*célsine*), by murdering his son they abandoned the duties following from their part in the social contract (*folud*).[38]

To translate in such a way is to recognize the existence of a gulf not only between languages but between cultural systems. In such discourses we see a remarkable level of international self-awareness, a recognition that the Irish language embeds an ideological system that forms an integrated whole. Hundreds of years later, in the very different world of post-Reformation controversy, Geoffrey Keating would argue that the law and custom of Gaelic Ireland should be understood not by looking at this or that custom in isolation, but by recognizing the integrity of the Irish system as a whole, respecting it as 'like a little world unto itself', *amhail domhan mbeag*.[39] This is the self-awareness of an Early Modern intellectual; but an equally radical sense of cultural relativism is already hinted at centuries earlier by the poetic voices of Blathmac and *Saltair na Rann*.

37 James Carney, 'Language and literature to 1169' in Ó Cróinín (ed.), *New History of Ireland Vol. 1*, 451–510, at pp. 496–7; cf. Brian Lambkin, *Studia Celtica* 20/21 (1985–6), 67–77.

38 Kelly, *Law*, 158–9.

39 Geoffrey Keating, *Foras Feasa ar Éirinn/ The History of Ireland*, vol. 1, ed. David Comyn (London: Irish Texts Society, 1901), 38.

The Graeco-Roman past in Middle Irish narrative

These poems bear comparison with a corpus that is superficially very different: the Middle Irish narrative cycle recreating Graeco-Roman military history and heroic myth.[40] This corpus developed gradually over at least five centuries. It is bracketed at one end by narratives of the Trojan war and the conquests of Alexander, *Togail Troí* and *Scéla Alexandair*, each composed by combining elements from disparate Latin texts from as early as the tenth century onward,[41] and at the other by *Stair Ercuil ocus a bás*, an account of Hercules most likely translated from the English of a printed work from Caxton's press – looking towards the mainstream Renaissance world, but in language and style embedded in a tradition stretching back to the time *Togail Troí* was composed.[42] From between these points in time we have an extraordinary range of texts, partly based on line-by-line translation and partly built up by embellishing the skeleton of the source texts with digressions and adornments freely composed or modelled on borrowings from elsewhere in the ancient sources.

40 Useful survey by Máire Ní Mhaonaigh, 'Classical compositions in medieval Ireland: the literary context', in *Translations from Classical Literature:* Imtheachta Aeniasa *and* Stair Ercuil ocus a bás, Irish Texts Society Subsidiary Series no. 17, ed. Kevin Murray (London: Irish Texts Society, 2006), 1–19.

41 Whitley H. Stokes (ed. and tr.), *Togail Troí from the Book of Leinster* (Calcutta, 1881) and *Togail Troí 1*, in id. and E.Windisch, *Irische Texte* vol. II.1 (Leipzig: S. Hirtzel, 1884), 1–141; Erich Peters, 'Die irische Alexandersage', *ZCP* 30 (1967), 71–264. On the dating of *Togail Troí* see the challenging proposal by Hildegard L.C. Tristram, 'The "Cattle-Raid of Cuailnge" in tension and transition between the oral and the written: classical subtexts and narrative heritage', in *Cultural Identity and Cultural Integration: Ireland and Europe in the Early Middle Ages*, ed. Doris Edel (Dublin: Four Courts Press, 1995), 61–81, with the forthcoming study by Brent Miles, *Heroic Saga and the Reception of Latin Epic in Medieval Ireland* (Cambridge: Boydell and Brewer, expected 2011).

42 See Erich Poppe, '*Stair Ercuil ocus a Bás* – rewriting Hercules in Ireland', in Murray (ed.), *Translations from Classical Literature*, 37–68.

Despite this variety, the corpus is stylistically homogeneous. Two distinct registers of literary Latin, dense prose narrative and hexameter verse with dislocated word order and subordinating syntax, are transferred to the high register of Irish prose in a 'jewelled style', heavy with alliteration and parallelism and deploying similes and other images in an arrangement that tends to be cumulative rather than architectonically structured. This is driven by a sustained and powerful effort: to transfer the source texts into the language, style and literary character typical of saga narrative on native Irish themes, most obviously *Táin Bó Cuailnge*[43] and the battle-narratives, *caithréimeanna*, of Middle Irish narrative eulogy.[44] In their context in the great manuscript compilations where they survive, the classicizing texts play a role complementary to the *Lebor Gabála* and the other documents of Irish pseudohistory. Where the *Lebor Gabála* inserts the antiquity and integrity of the Irish among the national histories of the world, the Classical sequence redefines the narratives of Graeco-Roman high storytelling as part of a cycle of authentically Irish lore.

Nowhere is this clearer than in *Togail Troí*, where the tradition's exuberant resources of simile and bombast evoke the wild excesses of the heroic age. When *Togail Troí* is set alongside *Táin Bó Cuailnge*, as is literally the case in the Book of Leinster, the two gain contextual meaning by the juxtaposition: the grotesquely primeval warlike world of Irish saga is given European resonance, as well as *vice versa*.[45] The translation dynamic becomes part of an overall vision of historical time, with the implicit assumption that the Irish and Classical narratives depict a remote pagan past that was

43 Miles, *Heroic Saga*, ch. 3.

44 Uáitéar Mac Gearailt, 'Togail Troí: ein Vorbild für spätmittelirische catha', in *Übersetzung, Adaptation und Akkulturation im insularen Mittelalter*, ed. H.L.C. Tristram and E. Poppe (Münster: Nodus Publikationen, 1999), 123–39; also '*Togail Troí*: an example of translating and editing in medieval Ireland', *Studia Hibernica* 31 (2000/2001) 71–86.

45 Michael Clarke, 'An Irish Achilles and a Greek Cú Chulainn', in *Ulidia II: Proceedings of the Second International Conference on the Ulster Cycle*, ed. Ruairí Ó hUiginn and Brian Ó Catháin (Maynooth: An Sagart, 2009), 271–84.

essentially similar at both ends of the world. It is significant that the *literati* set up explicit equivalences between the Irish and Classical names of demonic battle-spirits, who can be thought of as part of the pre-Christian landscape of pagan belief or placed among the hostile personalities familiar from the traditions of Christian monasticism.[46] In *Táin Bó Cuailnge* the Morrígu, the demon or goddess of battle who takes the form of an ominous bird, is famously equated with the Classical Fury Allecto,[47] while conversely in translating a Latin text about Allecto's sister Tisiphone the *literati* seize on the name of the Morrígu's sister, the Bodb.[48] This two-directional equivalence makes sense in terms of the logic that depicts the arrival of the Greek fleet at Troy in terms of the same series of riddling images as the approach of the Connacht host into Ulster (see below), and remodels the anticlimactic ending of Lucan's *Civil War* with an account of the encounter between Caesar and Pompey that uncannily echoes the combats between Ulster and Connacht heroes in the Ulster Cycle.[49]

46 See David Brakke, *Demons and the Making of the Monk: Spiritual Combat in Early Christianity* (Cambridge Mass.: Harvard University Press, 2006).

47 See Cecile O'Rahilly (ed. and tr.), *Táin Bó Cuailnge Recension I* (Dublin: Dublin Institute for Advanced Studies, 1976), line 995.

48 See George Calder (ed. and tr.), *Togail na Tebe: the Irish Version of the Thebaid of Statius* (Cambridge: Cambridge University Press, 1922), lines 4313–14, with the Latin original of Statius, *Thebaid* 11, 58–9. Similarly Allecto becomes the Bodb at *In Cath Catharda*, line 902, based on Lucan, *Civil War* 1.572–4 (Whitley Stokes (ed. and tr.), *In Cath Catharda*, in id. and E. Windisch, *Irische Texte* IV.2 (Leipzig: S. Hirtzel, 1909)). The parallelism is obvious between the two pairs of sisters – Allecto, Tisiphone, Megara and Morrígu, Macha, Bodb – and this presumably influenced the *literati* in setting up the parallel, or even in developing the Morrígu myth in the first place. See most recently Jacqueline Borsje, 'Demonising the enemy: a study of Congal Cáech', in J.E. Rekdal and A. Ó Corráin, ed., *Proceedings of the Eighth Symposium of Societas Celtologica Nordica* (Uppsala: Uppsala Universitet, 2007), 21–38.

49 *In Cath Catharda* 4660 ff., 5203ff.; and see in general John R. Harris, *Adaptations of Roman Epic in Medieval Ireland* (Lewiston: Edwin Mellon Press, 1998), 119–58.

Warrior fury: a Classical theme translated and recreated

Fundamentally, then, the warriors who are the main focus of these texts form a single class of men, whether they are Irishmen or Greeks or indeed Israelites. All belong to the same phase of a system of history whose overall pattern is of vitality decreasing over time. This point is made explicitly in *Cogadh Gaedhel re Gallaibh*, the twelfth-century panegyric history of Brian Boru, when the writer depicts the warlike brilliance of Brian's son Murchadh as a revival or emulation of the heroes of old – Conall Cernach from the Ulster Cycle, Troilus from the Trojan War, Samson from the Holy Land, and so on. He characterizes Murchadh as a throwback to an earlier state of humanity, a kind of heroic adolescence between the feebleness of the world's childhood and its modern decline into dotage: 'thus championship and the world are compared with human life, according to the intellectual comparison'.[50] Such a model helps to explain the air of wild bombast that characterizes the warriors' behaviour and the imagery applied to it. The underlying theme is an excess of energy – heroic, inspiring, admirable, but also potentially grotesque and exaggerated.

Characteristically, it is in the description of battle-fury that this finds its fullest expression. The most famous example is of course the *riastrad* or 'warp-spasm' of Cú Chulainn in *Táin Bó Cuailnge*:

> The torches of the Bodb, virulent rain-clouds and sparks of blazing fire, were seen in the air over his head with the seething of fierce rage (*re fiuchud na ferge fírgarge*) that rose in him. His hair curled about his head like branches of red hawthorn used to re-fence a gap in a hedge. If a noble apple-tree weighed down with fruit had been shaken about his hair, scarcely one apple would have reached the ground through it, but an apple would have stayed impaled on each separate hair because of the fierce bristling of the hair above his head. The warrior's moon (*lúan láith*) rose from his forehead, as long and as thick as a hero's fist and it was as long as his nose ... (Recension I, 2265–74, tr. O'Rahilly (slightly adapted); sim. lines 1651–6, by the H-interpolator)

50 *Cogadh Gaedhel re Gallaibh* in James Henthorn Todd (ed. and tr.), *The Irish Version of the Historia Brittonum of Nennius* (Dublin: Irish Archaeological Society, 1848), ch.117, pp. 186–7.

The image has become so familiar as a uniquely Irish, even Celtic, commonplace that it is easy to ignore the winder context from which it emerges. As I have discussed elsewhere,[51] an astonishingly close parallel is found in *Togail Troí*, where the young warrior Troilus undergoes an almost identical distortion:

> Ros-lín bruth 7 ferg, 7 ataracht an lon láich asa éton combó comfhota frisin sróin, 7 dodechatar a dí shúil asa chind combat sithithir artemh fria chenn anechtair. Ropo chuma a fholt 7 cróebrad scíad. Rofhóbair an cruthsin na slógu, amal léoman léir lán luind letharthaigh reithes do thruchu torcraide. (*Togail Troí 1*, 1471–88)
> [Fury and anger entered [Troilus]; and out of his forehead there rose the hero's moon until it was as long as his nose; and his two eyes came out of his head till they were longer than a hand's measure on the outside of his head. His hair was like the branches of a hawthorn. He attacked the hosts in this way like a violent lion, full of rending fury, who runs to attack a herd of boars.] (tr. Stokes, revised)

In terms of the translational dynamic that we have traced, it makes sense that the boy-warrior of the Trojans and the boy-warrior of the Ulstermen should undergo the same frenzy at the height of battle, and that it should be realized in the same system of imagery.

This way of conceptualizing the warrior's mental experience, as a surging or boiling of the spirit, is neatly indexed by words like *fiuchud* and especially *gal*. Each of these words sometimes invites translation as 'fury', sometimes as 'surging' or 'boiling' or even 'steam': and the apparent polysemy[52] hides the fact that the two things are conceptualized in terms of each other, as in a remarkable description of an advancing host in the Book of Leinster version of *Togail Troí*:

> Asrengsatar a nginchraesu. Ra boilgsetar a n-óli ... In gaeth dano dodechaid assa mbélaib 7 assa srónaib, is bec nara thrascair na thrénmiledu dara n-ais 7 na ruc a fultu dia forcléthib 7 nara shéit a ndechelta da n-airbrunnib. (*LL* 237a 49 ff)[53]

51 Clarke, 'An Irish Achilles and a Greek Cú Chulainn'.

52 See Myles Dillon, 'The semantic history of Irish *gal* "valour; steam"', *Celtica* 8 (1968), 196–200.

53 Text from Richard I. Best and Michael A. O'Brien, *The Book of Leninster* Vol. 4 (Dublin: Dublin Institute for Advanced Studies, 1965).

> [They drew out their jaws; they swelled their cheeks ... The wind also, that came out of their mouths and out of their nostrils, almost cast down the strong soldiers backwards and took the hair from the tops of their heads, and blew their cloaks from their breasts.] (tr. Stokes, revised)

This concept motivates a complex conceit found in near-identical form in *Togail Troí* and *Táin Bó Cuailnge*. A messenger uses a series of allusive descriptions to convey the vast and terrifying scale of the approaching forces of the enemy, and one by one he interprets their literal meanings. When he tells how he saw a great mist and vapour hanging in the air, it is interpreted in this way:

> In glasnél tiugaide atconnarc úasin ler, it hé anála na curad 7 na lath ngaile rolínsat dreich na fairge 7 a cobán fil etir nem 7 talmain, fobíthin frisrócaib in gal 7 fiuchiud na ferge faibraige i n-erbruinnib na láech lánchalma ... (*Togail Troí* 847–62)
> [The thick grey cloud, which I beheld over the sea, is the breaths of the heroes and the champions of valour (*lath ngaile*) that filled the face of the sea and the hollow which is between heaven and earth, because the surging (*gal*) and boiling (*fiuchud*) of the keen-edged wrath rose up in the breasts of the valiant heroes.] (tr. Stokes, revised)

This functions not only as a vivid visual image but also as a verbal riddle, playing on the semantic ambiguity: the fury of the warriors and the surging air are identified with each other, lexically as well as conceptually. It is typical of the configuration we have been observing that the same conceit (in almost exactly the same words) is equally appropriate for the Irish heroic age in *Táin Bó Cuailnge*, where Mac Roth and Fergus enact the exchange of image and interpretation.[54]

This theme of swelling breath in turn interacts closely with one that is embedded in the original narratives of Classical heroic lore. In Greek and Latin epic from Homer onward it is a recurring theme that the energy or spirit of the heroes shades from courage into reckless frenzy and ultimately into bestial madness; and this process is conceptualized in terms of the swelling and expansion of the mental or spiritual breath that surges in the

54 Lines 3558 ff. in O'Rahilly's edition.

warrior's breast.[55] In the translations, this system of imagery effectively merges with the Irish system based on boiling and surging. Witness a typically extravagant image in Statius' *Thebaid*:

> Tenet in capulis hastisque paratas
> Ira manus, animusque ultra thoracas anhelus
> Conatur, galeae tremunt horrore comarum (8.387 ff.)
> [Anger keeps their hands ready on hilt and spear, and the breast pants in effort beyond the corslet, helmets tremble with the rising of the hair.]

In Irish this becomes something quite different at the word-for-word level, but equivalent when the appropriate cross-cultural leap is made to the Irish conception of heroic swelling in the breast:

> Ros-lin fuailfed fergi fithigi coma hurloma lama na loechraidi do chlaidbib cruaidi cathaigthi 7 do slegaib seta sodibraicthi re hailgius na hirgaili (*Togail na Tebe* 3059–61)
> [A convulsion[56] of boiling rage filled them, so that the hands of the hero-folk were ready with heroic swords of war and with long well-casting spears for joy at the conflict.] (tr. Calder)

Similarly, in Lucan's *Civil War* the people of Massilia, besieged by Caesar, plead with him to turn aside his 'indomitable fury and harsh mind', *furorem/ indomitum duramque mentem* (3.304–5), and he responds in anger:

> turbato iam prodita voltu
> ira ducis tandem testata est voce dolorem (3.356–7).
> [The leader's anger, betrayed by his troubled face, at last found proof through his voice.]

In Irish this becomes another boiling of rage:

55 See for example Michael Clarke, *Flesh and Spirit in the Songs of Homer* (Oxford: Oxford University Press, 1999), ch.4; Christopher Gill, *Personality in Greek Epic, Tragedy and Philosophy* (Oxford: Oxford University Press, 1996), ch. 2; Barbara Graziosi and Johannes Haubold, 'Homeric Masculinity: ΗΝΟΡΕΗ and ΑΓΗΝΟΡΙΗ', *Journal of Hellenic Studies* 123 (2003) 60–76.

56 Notice that the same word is also used of turbulence in water.

> Ocus ro érigh ruithengris ádhbul 7 ruamnadh romór a ngnúis 7 a n-aigid Césair d'fhiuchudh na fergi fírgairbhi atracht in a mhenmain don aithesc sin ro raidhset na Masilecda fris. (*In Cath Catharda* 1685–7)
> [And a huge shining blaze and a great reddening rose on the face and visage of Caesar from the boiling (*fiuchudh*) of truly-rough anger that rose in his mind from that answer that the Massalians spoke to him.]

On a smaller scale, the image of surging breath emerges in the Irish rendering of Latin passages where the image is not even hinted at. Witness a description in Vergil's *Aeneid* of dust rising from the plain as an army advances:

> Hic subitam nigro glomerari pulvere nubem
> prospiciunt Teucri et tenebras insurgere campis (9.33–4)
> [Here the Teucri see a sudden cloud gathering in black dust, and darkness rising from the plains.]

In the Latin, this is simply the dust thrown up by the movement of men and horses; but in *Imtheachta Aeniasa*, the Irish version of the *Aeneid*,[57] the cloud is subsumed into the traditional image of rising breath:

> Robai dono nell duibchiach uaistib do luaithredh in talmun 7 do analaib na n-echradh 7 na laech batar forro in conair tancatar. (1979–80)
> [There was a cloud of dark mist over them, from the dust of the earth and from the breath of the horses and of the warriors that were on them, the way that they came.] (tr. Calder)

Here the visual logic of the original has been lost in the visual logic of Irish heroic narrative, and the absorption is complete.

This theme finds its most baroque expression in an image found many times in these texts, appropriate equally for ancient Irish and Graeco-Roman warriors. The surging and boiling of valour rises out of the warrior and a supernatural presence appears over his head, visualized as 'bird of valour'

57 George Calder (ed. and tr.), *Imtheachta Aeniasa/ The Irish Aeneid* (London: Irish Texts Society, 1907).

and sometimes, significantly, identified as a warlike divinity or spectre. I cite a fine example from the twelfth-century text *Fled Dún na nGéd*:[58]

> Ro ling dásacht 7 mire menman a Congal fri haithesc in óclaig sin 7 ro ling in fúir demnach .i. Tesifone a cumgaise a chride do chumniugad cecha drochchomairli dó. Ro érig didiu ina sheasam 7 ro gab a gaiscead fair 7 ro érig a bruth míled 7 a én gaile for folúamain úasa 7 ní tharat aichne for charait ná for nemcharait in tan sin ... (289–94)
> [At the young warrior's speech, wildness and frenzy of mind leapt onto Congal and the demonic Fury, Tisiphone, leapt into the closeness of his heart when he recalled all his bad advice. Then he rose into his standing and put his armour on himself, and his soldier's blazing rose up, and his bird of valour hovering over him, and he did not recognize friends or foes at that time.]

The presence of Tisiphone, one of the Latin names of the Furies, shows the affinitiy of the image with the Classical image of heroism. Compare an example in *Togail Troí*, where the equivalent Irish battle-spectres are named:

> ... coro eirgetar a n-eoin gaile ósa n-analaib, coro chomthócbaiset a lonna láith ósa cleithib ra fiuchud na ferggi fírgarbi. Atrachtadar badba bána béllethna osa cennaib ... (*LL* 239b 40ff, text from Best & O'Brien)
> [... their birds of ferocity arose from their breaths. Their warrior's moons sprang up from their breasts with the surging (*fiuchud*) of the right-fierce rage. Pale narrow-mouthed *badba* rose up over their heads ...] (tr. Stokes)

This image in turn is closely to comparable to one in the *Irish Aeneid*, describing Aeneas' furious reaction to the news that the youth Pallas has been killed:

> In tan tra rochuala Aenias in sgel sin, doerigh a bruth 7 a brig and, 7 a fherg 7 a ghal curudh, 7 adraig a en gaile co mbai for luamain uasa cind. (2567–8)
> [When Aeneas heard that story, his boiling and his force rose up there, and his anger and his warrior steam (*gal*), and his bird of ferocity rose up so that it was hovering over his head.] (tr. Calder)

58 Ruth Lehmann (ed.), *Fled Dúin na nGéd* (Dublin: Dublin Institute for Advanced Studies, 1964).

Intriguingly, however, this image is not in the Latin original: the Irish author, taking his cue apparently from the one word *ardens*, 'blazing', in Virgil's Latin (*Aeneid* 10.514), builds it up into a formulaic image belonging to his traditional stock.

In this way, the Irish texts follow a perspective depending on two allied notions: a general sense that the world was in something like childhood or adolescence when the heroic generations of Ireland and the Classical lands fought their wars, and the specific assumption that the characteristic mode of their existence was an exaggeration of energy, whether tending towards superhuman bravery or bizarre and grotesque excesses of violence. The imagery of swirling breath that we have observed is a particularly vivid example of this theme in action. But there is a final twist in the tale. In the very earliest Greek poetry articulating this theme, Homer's *Iliad*, the key word used for the swelling of warlike energy in the breast is *cholos*, which translates literally as 'bile'.[59] The medieval *literati* could not have read Homer directly, but the shadows of Homeric imagery are everywhere in the Latin epics that they did read. Remarkably, it has recently been shown that Greek *cholos* and Irish *gal* can be analysed as reflexes of the same Indo-European root word, reconstructed as **ghelh2-*.[60] There is every reason to think that elements of the accompanying imagery in the two traditions may go back to a single concept in the remote shared prehistory of the two languages. In itself this is no more than a curiosity: but it presents a striking example of the complex dynamics of cross-cultural translation. When the Irish created this extraordinary fusion between native and continental heroic lore in the articulation of a vision of the past, they were also reaching towards a primeval theme that had survived independently in the two traditions before it was recreated and developed anew in their pseudohistorical discourse. I offer this as a

59 Clarke, *Flesh and Spirit in the Songs of Homer*, ch. 4.

60 C.M. Driessen, 'Evidence for **ghelh2*, a new Indo-European root', *Journal of Indo-European Studies* 31 (2003), 279–305, Kim McCone,'Greek *Keltos* and *Galatos*, Latin *Gallus* "Gaul"', *Die Sprache* 46 (2006) 94–111.

suggestion that the traditions of translation which I have sketched in this chapter are much more than the by-product of the desire of peripheral nations to flow into the European mainstream: they are also the record of an adventure in comparative ethnology and, ultimately, of cultural self-understanding.

JOHN KINSELLA

East Meets West: Some Portuguese Translations of Eastern Poetry

The temporal connections and cultural interactions between the Iberian peninsula and the Eastern and Southern regions of Asia are parts of a process that became especially prominent in the fourteenth and fifteenth centuries as the European elites sought cotton from India and fine silks from China. Such enterprises were also informed by intellectual exchanges and theological dislocations of meaning that led to the distribution of new and intense proportions of significance. Out of the economic background flowed a vital theological system of values from the west, as the Jesuit initiatives of the fifteenth and sixteenth centuries were concentrated increasingly in India, China and Japan. Central to such initiatives was St Francis Xavier's journey to the East in 1542; he finally made his way to Japan in 1549 where he stayed until 1551. This provides an interesting example of cultural sensitivity and transition in a complex sequence of cultural exchanges and corresponding transmutations, since it was he who understood the crucial role played by language in the promulgation of missionary faith and its chain of significance in this very different world. He was convinced that cultural transformation of local belief systems could only be possible if the ideas of faith were incorporated into the supporting structures of the local languages. For this reason he exhorted his companions to learn local languages both as a pragmatic exercise in and for itself and in the acknowledgement of intercultural dialogue with all its inherent ethical and religious concerns.

Luís Fróis has some apposite words on this particular matter in his *Historia de Japam*:

> No tempo estiverão em Cagoxima, aonde começarão a lançar logo os primeiros fundamentos da fé, padecião grande detrimento na carência da língua da qual não sabião ainda mais que o que particularmente o Irmão João Fernandes vinha da India aprendendo com aqueles japões. A maior parte do dia se ocupavam na comunicação dos próximos, e de noite prolongavão suas vigilias em oração, e um rudimento da língua com grande instância.
> [During the time they were in Kagoshima, where they started to promulgate the first foundations of their faith, they were greatly hampered by their linguistic shortfallings in their exchanges with others of which they only knew what Brother João Fernandes had learnt from the Japanese in India. They spent most of their days speaking to their neighbours and at night spent their time in vigilant prayer, assiduously studying the basic rudiments of the language.][1]

The learning of the Japanese language is thus recognized as a deep anchor for the Jesuit mission which is later confirmed by Padre Costa de Torres who was the superior between 1549 and 1560. Evidently the nature of the task was highly regarded: it is worth considering the case of João Fernandes, who insisted on speaking Japanese and would speak Portuguese 'nem com os Padres nem com os Irmãos novos que vinhão da India [neither with the Fathers nor with the new Brothers recently arrived from India]'.[2] This is certainly an early case of devotion to duty in relation to the advantages of linguistic immersion in terms of the understanding of the Other and related cultural phenomena.

When the Jesuits were later to treat with the highly sophisticated culture of China with its printing presses and advanced educational system, they went as far as to translate European books into the Chinese languages in spite of the enormous difficulties of the task and their recognition of the reluctance of the Chinese court to read foreign works. It might be added

1 Luís Fróis, S.J., *História de Japam*, 5 vols. Annotated edition of José Wicki, S.J. Lisbon, National Library, 1976–1984. Vol. 1., 217–18. Cited by Ana Paula Laborinho on p. 7 of her excellent paper 'Da descoberta dos povos ao encontro das línguas: o português como lingual intermediária a Oriente', given at a conference on Latin Humanism and the Cultures of the Far East, Macau, 6–8 January 2005. Available online at http://www.humanismolatino.online.pt/v1/pdd/C003-010.pdf. Accessed 24 June 2010. All translations into English in what follows in this article are by J.K.

2 Ana Paula Laborinho, 8.

that such an initiative was more effective and less challenging than the alternative of attempting to persuade their interlocutors to read texts in the original Latin. These translation efforts represent an important attempt at dialogue on the part of the Jesuits at this imperialist conjunction of Iberian history, notwithstanding their obvious religious motivations that accompanied the European dislocations at the time.

In the case of Portugal, this small kingdom appeared insignificant on the European map but its own dispersions led to settlements in Southern and Eastern Asia as well as Africa. The Estado da India stretched all the way from Sofala and Hormuz and the first *feitoria* or trading post in the East was established in Calicut in 1506, whilst a long and historical association with China dates back to the sixteenth century when the imperial ridge of Macau was developed on the edges of this vast territorial space. Early European visitors to the settlement included Portugal's best known literary figure, Luis de Camões, whose major work *Os Lusíadas* reveals a climate in which 'direct contact with and experience of foreign cultures engendered a more dialogistic relationship with "Otherness", although Camões was as ethnocentric as many diehard imperialists'.[3] Influenced by the utopian thinking of Tomé Pires and others, there was also a tendency to portray Otherness in terms of qualities not available in the home culture. There is no doubt that Camões was reacting according to a particular period and society with its own specific beliefs and superstitions, its own myths and legends. Yet in spite of the imperialist attitudes so apparent in the *Lusiads*, it is not insignificant that there also exists a certain admiration for aspects of China even when they were frequently based on erroneous understandings of the culture itself. Another traveller to China and Japan was Fervão Mendes Pinto whose work *Peregrinação* was also influenced by Tomé Pires, evoking serious divergences between the avarice and corruption of Europe as opposed to the greater sense of moral and spiritual harmony apparent in China. It is not axiomatic, therefore, that the imperial experience was portrayed through a totally Manichean paradigm.

3 David Brookshaw and Clive Willis, 'Introduction', *Lusophone Studies* 1 (Bristol: Bristol University, 2000), ii.

The Chinese thinker Zhang Longxi has produced a fascinating and seminal text that serves as a response to the sort of stereotyping to which we have alluded and offers a useful revision of such distorted and false perceptions. His refounding of this issue is summarized in a section that reads as follows:

> In the fusion of horizons, we are able to transcend the boundaries of language and culture so that there is no longer isolation of East and West – no longer the exotic, mystifying, inexplicable Other, but something to be learned and assimilated until it becomes part of our knowledge and experience of the world. Thus, in demythologising China as the myth of the Other, the myth disappears but not the beauty, for the real differences between China and the West will be fully recognized and China's true other will be appreciated as contributing to the variety of our world and the totality of what we may still proudly call the heritage of human culture.[4]

It is in the spirit of the parameters expressed here that interested researchers and scholars might elicit some shared foundation of mutual correspondence for engaging with the divergences that emerge in discussion of East and West. The work of Zhang Longxi has certainly transformed the theory and practice and also demonstrates the exceptional resonances of the authentic comprehension of both variety and universality, of oppositions and convergences in ways of perceiving the world. One consequence of this for the reader or translator is the sense of involvement in a two-way journey that can provide an 'opening towards alternative versions of universality that are wrought from the work of translation itself'.[5]

The interlocking relation between the western translation and a text of eastern origin can thus be regarded as an exhilarating and liberating dimension, where the original is both retrieved and restored or re-created in all of its freshness. The upshot of this translation work should be the establishment of a type of world poetry in which, as Stephen Owen indicates, the

4 Zhang Longxi, *Mighty Opposites: from Dichotomies to Difference in the Comparative Study of China* (Stanford: Stanford University Press, 1998), 54.

5 Judith Butler, 'Competing Universalities', in *Contingency, Hegemony, Universality: Contemporary Dialogues on the Left*, ed. Judith Butler, Ernesto Laclau and Slavoj Zizek (London: Verso, 2000), 136–81.

translator is able to 'create interesting approximations, to point directions, to give echoes, to construct families of differences'.[6] In this way translation does not destroy the original as it attempts to catch hold of its substance of feeling, and it will enable itself to be faithful to its mission of enhancing our appreciation of different merits as well as our participation in a quest for different but shared values.

This issue is most significant in relation to poetry itself and offers a connection with Zhang Longxi's supremely important proclamations. Indeed Owen does not seek to abolish or evade the differences, maintaining quite simply that 'Chinese poetry is not "other" but "unfamiliar"'. Owen refuses to invite a simplistic form of either uniformity or insuperable distance and acts as a pivotal guide in any scrutiny of more recent twentieth-century translations and their appeal and acceptance as a genre of poetry following Eastern models or as poems translated into Portuguese and Spanish.

It is important to note that the process of reciprocal cultivation and imperialist constructs of imagination continued to flourish even as the Western powers followed the compelling demands of capitalist economics, engineering the hierarchical policies of their imperial nationalisms. Within the ominous context of the increasingly dangerous world of the late nineteenth and the twentieth century together with the political, economic and cultural concerns of World War, the interest in Eastern cultural values remained. The power of language and human imagination was such that there was still room for some type of dialogue in spite of the derangements and perversions wrought by the political and technological monologism of the West's destructive capacities. Given the uncompromising nature of such distortions, all successes are to be applauded insofar as they moisten the ground of intercultural embrace and irrigate the wasteland of the human soul in times of disjunction and deep anxiety.

6 Stephen Owen, cited by Roslyn Joy Ricci in her paper, 'Lost in Translation or gained in Creation: Classical Chinese Poetry Re-Created as English Poetry', given at the 15th Biennial Conference of the Asian Studies Association of Australia, Canberra, 29 June–2 July 2004. This work provided a very useful perspective for my own understanding of translating from Chinese poetry into Portuguese.

In appraising and asserting the viable efforts made within the Lusophone world, interesting works were much later to emerge from the mid-Atlantic margins of the Madeiran and Azorean archipelagos with the works of Herberto Helder and Emanuel Félix. One of the more cogent features of both Helder's versions of Zen poems, his Japanese peasant songs and Emanuel Félix's arrangements of Chinese and Japanese poems, is the sense of reverence displayed together with a recognition of a certain resilience in the classical beauty of the poetry reproduced in Portuguese. This is what opens up a path from the tiny island of Terceira in the Azores or Madeira and turns it into an exhilarating journey that allows for an authentic dialogue with a millennial culture and sets the stage for works of translation that interface with the Oriental world in an endeavour of both cultural and temporal interpretation.

In the case of the Chinese poets, moreover, there are important ingredients that disclose a deep understanding of the connection between human emotion and the natural landscape in such a way as to make the natural world a space for the disclosure of human emotion. However, the associations and assumptions of image and metaphor cannot be immediately presumed in any undertaking of this sort. For example, the magpie in China is linked to happiness whilst the crane was viewed as a magical bird that is linked to a long life and Taoist sorcery.[7] Yet while such metaphors may not readily cross cultural boundaries without a moderate amount of explanation of the human experiences that lie behind them, it is also important to consider that the crossing of cultural and temporal boundaries is possible.

The haikus and Zen poems of Helder are remarkable for their freshness and vitality, retrieving and incorporating an elusive sense of integrity and richness from the originals in a highly concise language. An example of this activity is clear in the following poems:[8]

7 Greg Whincup, *The Heart of Chinese Poetry: China's Greatest Poems Newly Translated* (New York: Doubleday, 1987), 109.

8 Herberto Helder, *Poesia Toda* (Lisbon: Assírio & Alvim, 1990), 219.

Ervas do estio
lugar onde os guerreiros
Sonham.

Um cuco
foge a longe – e ao longe
uma ilha.

Primeira neve
Bastante para vergar as folhas
Dos junquilhos.

[Summer grass,
A place where warriors
dream.

A cuckoo
Flies far away – and far away
an island.

The first snows:
enough to subdue the leaves
of the bull rushes.]

There is a sense of experience shared across vast boundaries and meaning recovered through poetic zest and immediacy; a feeling of stillness and beauty is transmitted as the distance of time and space is unveiled in a palpable recognition of Nature itself. In the case of Félix's translations the reader needs to know that his recreations of poets such as Wang Yan are based on French translations which are themselves versions of an original Chinese that itself gives prominence to verbal economy, cherishing the exact or singular image.

It is worth recalling that Chinese uses graphs and concepts such as 'xin' where the word for 'heart-mind' also has connotations of 'living up to one's word', an important Confucian notion where the idea of living up to one's word is a sign of a genuine heart-mind or a way of being on the right track. Finally, the Chinese sense of order is more aesthetic than rational and there is more difficulty in putting emotion and reason together.

Notwithstanding such concepts of otherness or difference, there is a unifying thread of human experience that carries across from one environment to the other, a common core that links the cultures in a dynamic of interactive patterns. Thus the concrete or the particular contribute to an understanding of wholeness.

This natural theme is especially present in Félix's '14 Poemas Chineses/14 Chinese Poems', but in an altogether different way.[9] In 'O Pescador/The Fisherman' there is a timeless rather than a cyclical quality, a serenity in relation to natural disaster: 'manobra o seu barco Que os canaviais floresçam ou sequem!/ and handles his boat Whether the cane fields flourish or grow dry'.[10] There is a hermetic and oblique tone present in this treatment of the passing of time whilst the proximity of nature serves as a pretext for speculation as the human strains are banished in favour of a sense of quiet fulfilment and completion. 'A Rapariga Pobre/The Poor Young Girl'[11] is reminiscent in some ways of Camilo Pessanha's 'Ao Longe Os Barcos de Flores/In the distance the boats of flowers', although Pessanha veered towards a more popular tradition and to the great poetry of understatement, the Chinese. Though the boats in question here are in point of fact floating brothels, the poet is able to detect the otherworldly sound of a flute, a symbol both of poetry and of an ideal: 'incessante, um som de flauta chora .../an incessant sound of the flute cries ....'[12] However, these are more jarring and disconcerting features in 'A Rapariga Pobre/The Poor Young Girl' or in 'A Beldade/The Beauty', which offer some indirect comments on the injustice of the world. For there is a price to be paid for the privileges of beauty and power:[13]

9 Emanuel Félix, *The Possible Journey: Poems 1965–1992*, trans. John M. Kinsella (Gavea-Brown: Providence, 2002), 125–54. All references are to this collection.

10 Félix, *The Possible Journey*, 126–7.

11 Emanuel Félix, *The Possible Journey*, 128–9.

12 Camilo Pessanha, *Obras de Camilo Pessanha: Clepsidra e Poemas Dispersos*, vol. 1 (Mem Martins: Publicações Europa-America, 1988), 95.

13 Emanuel Félix, *The Possible Journey*, 144–5.

Sabeis que as travessas do seu cabelo
São todos os impostos de muitas aldeias?
[You know that the side-combs of her hair
Are worth all the taxes of many villages?]

These poems are remarkable, not simply for their sense of serenity and peace (in spite of natural disaster and human injustice), but for the manner through which this is achieved; a recognition of time and its effects, the practice of acceptance as opposed to resistance, of things being in their right place. There are genuine tensions and risks present in the world but they are absorbed and exorcised through work and quiet meditation as illustrated in the 'Canção do Jang/The Jang's song':

Trabalho quando o sol se ergue,
Repouso quando ele se deita.
[I work when the sun rises,
I rest when it sets.]

These Chinese and Japanese poems collectively create a concentration of succinctly written work which makes the oriental tradition more amenable to a European reader. They also bear witness to Félix's dual undertaking as both poet and translator.

Translating, for Félix, is a way of reproducing a dialogue with a culture unknown to many readers. Although there has been a long history of Portuguese involvement in both China and Japan, there is a considerable gap between them, a distinction heightened by the time period of poems which testify to an underlying sense of the transience of human history. This rendering of Chinese poems by way of the Portuguese transports us into another land: in this case, into that delicate balance between the human and the natural that is the hallmark of Chinese civilization at its very best. As Professors Hall and Ames point out in the authoritative study, *Thinking from The Han*, Chinese sensibility fixes on the particular to express the joinings that build up universal worlds.[14] In stressing the

14 David Hall and Roger Ames, *Thinking from the Han* (Albany: State University of New York Press, 1998), 103–20.

way of 'thisness' the Chinese poetry summons up a strangely beautiful mood of odd but compelling transitions. It is this primacy of feeling that Félix evokes in his interpretations. As discussed previously, the Chinese speak of the 'heart-mind' – never just the mind – and these poems make clear why such a hybrid organ is at the centre of their cultural world. From nature to psyche, from sadness to elation, from sexual slavery to beauty, all these abrupt changes express a mood of felt unity. Félix conducts us into the rich realm of Chinese poetry with the sure and deft hand of an artist at work.

The difficulties faced by Félix in these translations are also relevant to the task faced in my own translations of his work into English. The aim of the translator is to recognize a feeling of unsettling strangeness or unfamiliarity and face up to the recalcitrance of the poetic expression. What is required is retrieval of the sense of cultural otherness, the linguistic differences, whilst retaining a fidelity to the original language. However, this provides an arena of conflicting tensions because of the irreducibility of certain linguistic or cultural differences, the failure to transform and heal the gaps. For example it was virtually impossible to capture the assonances of Portuguese sounds related to the sea. It is also difficult to negotiate linguistic and cultural diversity in love poems such as 'Breve Poema da tua Boca/Short Poem from Your Mouth', 'Porque não Partimos/ Why don't we Leave', or 'Melibeia', because of cultural difference.

It would be profitable to cite a remark by Michael Hamburger in relation to this problem: 'It is the plainest, most limpid poem that may defy translation, because it leaves the least latitude for paraphrase and interpretation, and the plainest that may be a happy reduction in one language and literary convention can sound like an intolerable banality in another'.[15] Polysyllabic words like 'sonriso' and 'Primavera' in Portuguese sound so abrupt and curt in the monosyllabic English equivalents of 'smile' and 'Spring'. Furthermore, within the push and pull of translations, the way in which emotions are encoded in language and the transmission of temperamental reverberations within cultures is another very thorny issue.

15 Michael Hamburger, 'On Translation', *PN Review* 16, 1980.

One culture may not externalize its feelings as much as another so that it becomes quite difficult to bridge the gap between the two. The reader may become aware of the semantic and phonic challenges of linguistic difference, the way in which language channels feelings and emotion in a very distinctive fashion. In the specific case of the neo-Latin languages this goes back to cultural traditions, the far greater strength of the classical rhetorical tradition of the Latin-based cultures, and the impact of the Baroque. These factors of course offer a powerful contrast at times where the more mellifluous sounds of the Portuguese versions of a poem clash with the English.

As a result of such endemic problems the translator often becomes aware of the pretence of trying to produce the exact poem in another language, vacillating between the semantic and phonic qualities and at other times looking both ways at once. There is perhaps something unsatisfying about any attempt to capture the inner circle of meanings to be found in a poem and then to transmit these inner workings to another tongue. An example of this is the poem 'Grilos/Crickets' where there is no English equivalent for the complex, etymological play of meaning that is central to the whole poem. Moreover, in pursuing this thread of meaning it also becomes clear that there are additional problems in translating a poem for the first time into English and introducing it to English-speaking culture. I cannot think of a better way of explaining these circumstances than a citation by Antoine Berman who remarks that,

> parce que toute première traduction, ... est imparfaite et, pour ainsi dire, impure: imparfaite, parce que la défectivité traductive et l'impact des 'normes' s'y manifestent souvent massivement, impure parce qu'elle est à la fois introduction et traduction. [Since every first translation, ... is imperfect and, so to speak impure: imperfect, because the defects of translation and the impact of the 'norms' are very frequently to be found at a fundamental level, impure because it is both introduction and translation.][16]

16 Antoine Berman, *Pour une critique des traductions: John Donne* (Paris: Gallimard, 1995), 84.

It is as a translator that I write these words and recognize that my own first translations of poets such as Herberto Helder and Emanuel Félix stand at the axis of a long relationship between distinct latitudes and cultures. What can finally be achieved in a sense of dialogue (through translation) is perhaps an intermediate world of unusual juxtapositions, of opposites and yet again a space for creativity. It is in this realm of the human imagination that there emerges a contrast between the authentic and its potential within a landscape of alternative visions, interpretations, associations and connections: a spirit of otherness is both transmitted and even transcended in a journey that can finally share a common axis.

CORMAC Ó CUILLEANÁIN

Channelling Emotions, Eliciting Responses: Translation as Performance

The present essay sets out to reflect on how translators can approach the task of transmitting emotional content and effects. This theme will be explored on the assumption that translation is, among other things, something of a performing art, and that performers are compelled, in many circumstances, to take personal ownership of each work they transmit, whether this is a song, a speech or a written text. Especially in cases of creative or personal communication, the translator or interpreter must convey a sense not only of what was said but also of how, where and why it was said, who said it, and what effect was anticipated. While the weighting of these various questions will be affected by the purposes and intended readership of the translated text, the solutions adopted must originate from the source text, or bear a meaningful relation to it; otherwise we would not be dealing at all with translation as a specific activity. The process of transmission is not always straightforward: some of the elements that constitute the message may be implied rather than contained in the source text, and some may be hard to trace and to define.

If the present discussion appears undisciplined or opinionated in places, this may be partially excused by the consideration that in discussing emotion at the level of detailed example, some element of subjectivity is inescapable, as emotional responses are personal, spontaneous and non-transferable. They may be prompted rather than prescribed. The impulse towards tears or laughter lies partly outside the control of the rational mind.[1]

1 Dante, in *Purgatorio* canto 25, represents himself as struggling to contain a smile in a humorous situation. He fails, because (verses 106–8) 'riso e pianto son tanto seguaci

On emotional aspects of communication, Roman Jakobson writes that 'the emotive function ... flavors to some extent all our utterances, on their phonic, grammatical, and lexical level. If we analyze language from the standpoint of the information it carries, we cannot restrict the notion of information to the cognitive aspect of language'.[2] For the purposes of thinking about translation, it follows from this that, apart from those professional situations where a translator or interpreter is professionally obliged to adopt a neutral, non-expressive stance, the pressure of personal feeling must be accounted for in the translated version, in order to provide an adequate account of the text as a communicative act.

In his 'Closing Statement on Linguistics and Poetics', Jakobson famously outlined six 'factors inalienably involved in verbal communication':[3]

	CONTEXT	
ADDRESSER	MESSAGE	ADDRESSEE
	CONTACT	
	CODE	

These factors correspond to six functions which attend a communicative act:

/ a la passion di che ciascun si spicca, / che men seguon voler ne' più veraci' ('for tears and smiles are both so faithful to / the feelings that have prompted them that true / feeling escapes the will that would subdue'). See *The Divine Comedy of Dante Alighieri*, trans. Allen Mandelbaum (Berkeley and London: University of California Press, 1982) vol. 2 *Purgatorio*, 186. A (non-)translation joke told by the late Frank Muir illustrates, *per absurdum*, the non-transferability of amusement. An Englishman was being led through the Vatican Museum by his Italian interpreter. They came to a narrow corridor where the way was blocked by a group of Italians whose guide was a small cheerful Italian Monsignor. This man's descriptions and anecdotes kept his listeners in constant fits of merriment. The Englishman joined in the laughter. 'But I thought you knew no Italian', his interpreter objected. Pointing at the Monsignor, the Englishman replied: 'I trusted him'.

2 Roman Jakobson, 'Closing Statement: Linguistics and Poetics', in *Style in Language*, ed. Thomas A. Sebeok (Cambridge, Mass.: M.I.T. Press, 1960), 350–77 (pp. 353–4).

3 Jakobson, 'Closing Statement', 353, 357.

	REFERENTIAL	
EMOTIVE	POETIC	CONATIVE
	PHATIC	
	METALINGUAL	

Reading Jakobson's diagrams from left to right would give pride of place to the emotive function, connected with the person or entity initiating the communication. The emotive is connected with the role of the addresser.[4] The relative weight of the six functions is of course variable, but a prominent role for the emotive aspect seems particularly apt when considering performable texts. The interpreting branch of the translating profession will remind us most forcefully of the analogies between translation and performance noted at the start of this essay: musicians, actors and speakers are all, in their way, translators.[5]

If an interlingual interpreter is performing in the same space and at the same time as the original speaker, then a decision not to mimic the emotional style of the speaker's delivery would be a marked difference, and one that would be noticed by an attentive audience, although the actual information loss might be minimal if the spectators were able to gauge the original emotion through the channel of the original utterance.[6] The

4 We must distinguish the expression of emotion from the production of emotion. Obviously, extreme emotion can be produced in the listener by coldly and unemotionally announcing an item of painful news. But this is not a transfer of an emotion existing within the original utterance, and consequently does not form part of the present discussion of how translators can render the emotions contained in texts.

5 The same may apply to writers, as Proust realized: 'Je m'apercevais que ce livre essentiel, le seul livre vrai, un grand écrivain n'a pas, dans le sens courant, à l'inventer puisqu'il existe déjà en chacun de nous, mais à le traduire. Le devoir et la tâche d'un écrivain sont ceux d'un traducteur.' See Richard Bales, *Proust: A la recherche du temps perdu* (London, Grant & Cutler, 1995), 75. The translation process lends itself to metaphorical extension covering many processes of equivalence or metamorphosis: for example, it could plausibly embrace the assertion, often attributed to Paul Erdös, that a mathematician is a machine for converting coffee into theorems. I will stick mostly to texts in the present discussion.

6 Sometimes it may be appropriate for the interpreter to remain neutral even if the original speaker is emotional: for example, in translating a victim impact statement

case becomes more complex and intriguing when the originator and the translator are separated in space and time, and the translator or interpreter wishing to capture the emotive impulse of the text must work by empathy and conjecture in reconstructing an emotion which, in itself, is extra-textual, although it will probably have left traces in the message.[7]

In order to be translated, certain texts requiring a focus on the 'addresser' (such as literary dialogue) have to be actualized in the translator's mind, as a virtual performance, with imagined people generating or receiving the impact of what is said, particularly including the emotional impact. The translator may make mistakes in voicing the speakers, but to refuse to imagine the speakers in their interpersonal exchanges would be an obvious abdication of the task. Many other text types can also be performed, or experienced, in different ways and their contextual meaning and emotional impact may derive largely from effects which are not strictly text-based, or which cannot be directly produced by the words in the text. Methods of conveying attitude or emotion without leaving a trace on the written record could include the sarcastic adoption of a particular intonation, a slowed speed of enunciation, even a raised eyebrow. A compliment can become an insult; a judge's apparently scrupulous summing-up, entirely innocent on the written page, can sink the defendant under waves of irony. Important

at the end of a trial, where the injured party is entitled to be emotional while the court must remain balanced and objective.

7 Performance can also legitimately invest a text with attitudes not intended by its speaker, but justified by contextual factors: for example, a reading or performance of a text, in a tone that undermines its intended effect, may evoke derision or indignation among the listeners. A recent performance of Shakespeare's *The Taming of the Shrew* by the Rough Magic Theatre Company in Dublin subverted its misogynistic message while scrupulously relaying every word of the text. This was, in theatre terms, an enactment parallel to the Borges tale of Pierre Menard, who invented a whole new work in the same words as its earlier exemplar: 'his aim was never to produce a mechanical transcription of the original; he did not propose to copy it [but] to produce pages which would coincide – word for word and line for line – with those of Miguel de Cervantes'. See 'Pierre Menard, Author of Don Quixote', trans. Anthony Bonner, in Jorge Luis Borges, *Fictions*, ed. Anthony Kerrigan (London: John Calder, 1965), 42–51 (p. 45).

emotive effects cannot always be stated explicitly; indeed, explicitness can kill the intended effect. As J.L. Austin pointed out, 'I insult you' is not a felicitous speech act.[8] A neat illustration of this point comes from the film *Monty Python and the Holy Grail*, where a French knight's attempt to be offensive includes such memorable phrases as 'Your mother was a hamster and your father smelt of elderberries! … Now go away or I shall taunt you a second time!' The first sentence misfires, while the second shows how not to do things with words.

Translators, then, must deal with ambiguities and information gaps, while getting on with their ineluctable task. In order to visualize a working approach to the question of translating emotion, it may be helpful to look across a range of different translation types – interlingual, intralingual or intersemiotic – and different media – gesture, spoken word and written word – while always acknowledging the limits of the wordsmith's role in conveying emotional effects in a new language, especially when it was not necessarily conveyed through the original language. For although emotion has to do with thoughts and feelings, these are not always crystallized in words. It has been pointed out that one cannot experience the emotion of hunger, only the physical pain of hunger.[9] Emotion involves

8 Except, apparently, in Germany, where J.L. Austin records that 'in the hey-day of student duelling … it was the custom for members of one club to march past members of a rival club, each drawn up in file, and then for each to say to his chosen opponent as he passed, quite politely, "Beleidigung", which means "I insult you"'. J.L. Austin, *How To Do Things With Words*, ed. J.O. Urmson and Marina Sbisà, 2nd edn (Oxford: Oxford University Press, 1976), 30–1.

9 'The English word *emotion* combines in its meaning a reference to "feeling", a reference to "thinking", and a reference to a person's body. For example, one can talk about a "feeling of hunger", or a "feeling of heartburn", but not about an "emotion of hunger" or an "emotion of heartburn", because the feelings in question are not thought-related. One can also talk about a "feeling of loneliness" or a "feeling of alienation", but not an "emotion of loneliness" or an "emotion of alienation", because while these feelings are clearly related to thoughts (such as "I am all alone", "I don't belong", etc.), they do not suggest any associated bodily events or processes'. See Anna Wierzbicka, *Emotions Across Languages and Cultures: Diversity and Universals* (Cambridge: Cambridge University Press, 1999), 2.

the attitudes and values of its subject. It can be conveyed in many ways; there are cultural and intercultural gestures and expressions – even animal ones – denoting contempt, surprise, fear, shame and other reactions; these can be explained and described in words, but they are not themselves verbal phenomena.[10]

Of course these gestures can be translated across cultures, which may involve rewording the verbal descriptions in a new language or even, if necessary, altering the action described. Eugene A. Nida noted a problem with translating literally the parable of the Pharisee and the publican, where the humble sinner, overcome by remorse, beats his breast at the back of the temple. In some cultures, beating one's breast is a sign not of humility but of boastfulness, and therefore, when translating into one of those languages, beating his breast must be translated into the gesture of striking one's head, which is physically different but culturally and emotionally equivalent.[11]

Gaps remain, however, even within the basic categories of feeling whose equivalence one may be seeking through translation. Stanislaw Baranczak points out that the Polish word for 'happy' does not map onto the American word 'happy', simply because it has a much more restricted meaning and usage: 'it is generally reserved for rare states of profound bliss, or total satisfaction with serious things such as love, family, the meaning of life, and so on. ... What I'm trying to point out is only one example of the semantic

10 Charles Darwin examined the relationship between physical and cultural factors in his study, *The Expression of the Emotions in Man and Animals* (1882), interpreting physical data through a conceptual and therefore verbal framework.

11 'Whereas for some people translating may be primarily a matter of theoretical interest, the Bible translator must face up to certain immediate problems. For example, if he attempts to take literally the expression "he beat his breast" (speaking of the repentant Publican, Luke 18:13), he may discover that, as in the Chokwe language of Central Africa, this phrase actually means "to congratulate oneself" (the equivalent of our "pat himself on the back"). In some instances it is necessary to say "to club one's head"'. Eugene Nida, 'Principles of Translation as Exemplified by Bible Translating', in *On Translation*, ed. Reuben A. Brower (Cambridge, Mass.: Harvard University Press, 1959), 11–31 (pp. 11–12).

incompatibilities which are so firmly ingrained in languages and cultures that they sometimes make mutual communication impossible'.[12]

Happily, the focus of the present essay is narrower than the cultural correspondence of entire cultures; my focus is simply on the individual translator striving to elicit or prompt emotions in a putative reader or listener, more specifically in cases where there is a perceived continuity between the orginal utterer's emotions, those discernible in its translated equivalent, and those of the final receptors. The translator stands somewhere in the middle of a chain of signification and feeling, acting the roles of reader and writer, recreator and responder. In texts where such an unbroken chain of emotion is to be established, the assumption must be that the original speaker expresses emotion because he or she genuinely feels emotion, or convincingly pretends to do so. That means that the speaker in some sense owns the emotion, that it lies at the origins of the source text, and that the effect on the reader is a personal response to the originator's primordial feelings. It is hard to imagine a fellow human as a mover unmoved, so if the reader or listener is moved, then this is assumed to be, at the simplest level a case of sheer pre-rational sympathy with the originator of the message. In the case of auditory texts, as we all know from listening to emotive voices, we sense the feeling even before we have decoded the first word.

In the middle of the chain stands the translator, explaining in a different language what *I* feel. But who am *I* in this case? Is the translator entitled, or obliged, to assume ownership of the original emotion? The question becomes clearer when one moves from written to spoken translation, and is brought into sharper focus when music accompanies or replaces a text, in the process of intersemiotic translation defined by Roman Jakobson.[13] Sometimes the words of the source text accompany the music, in the original or in translation – but there is a sizeable body of opinion, not least in relation to grand opera, that the highest form of appreciation is to lose

12 Stanislaw Baranczak, *Breathing Under Water and other East European Essays* (Cambridge, Mass. and London: Harvard University Press, 1990), 13, quoted in Wierzbicka, *Emotions Across Languages and Cultures*, 248.

13 Roman Jakobson, 'Linguistic Aspects of Translation', in *On Translation*, ed. by Reuben A. Brower, 232–9 (p. 233, p. 238).

oneself in the music, following the sounds rather than the meanings of the words, and that we are as well off not knowing exactly what is being said by those 'over-upholstered females complaining noisily in foreign languages to or about their scandalously unromantic-looking lovers'.[14] This is not an entirely risible opinion, but I shall press on with at least one example of interlingual translation, if only to suggest that the parallel process of intersemiotic translation may be more fundamental, at least on the level of emotion. Shostakovich's 1934 opera *Lady Macbeth of Mtsensk* tells the highly upsetting story of a woman who murders her father-in-law and then her husband, so that she can be with her lover Sergei, who collaborates in the second murder. Both are convicted of their crime and dispatched to a life of forced labour; as they trudge across the steppes towards their destination, Sergei blames her for the murders, and then betrays her with another female convict, provoking her suicide.

At the outset of this final confrontation during the convicts' long march into the wilderness, the protagonist approaches her lover affectionately:

EKATERINA LVOVNA:
Seryózha! Khoróshy moy!
(She snuggles up to Sergey. Sergey maintains a sullen silence)
Nakonyéts-to!
Vyed' tsély dyen s tobóy nye videlas.
Seryózha!

14 Henry W. Simon and Abraham Veinus, *The Pocket Book of Great Operas* (New York: Pocket Books, 1949), vii. Another deterrent to translation may be the banality of some texts which have been sublimely set to music. For example, Richard Strauss's magnificent 'Morgen!' (Opus 27 no. 4) was inspired by a poem written in German by John Henry Mackay, which was translated into English as follows: 'Tomorrow's sun will rise in glory beaming, / And in the pathway that my foot shall wander, / We'll meet, forget the earth, and lost in dreaming, / Let heav'n unite a love that earth no more shall sunder ... / And towards that shore, its billows softly flowing, / Our hands entwined, our footsteps slowly wending, / Gaze in each other's eyes in love's soft splendour glowing, / Mute with tears of joy and bliss ne'er ending ...'. English edition of the song by John Bernhoff, 1925 Universal-Edition, reproduced on Wikipedia: en.wikipedia.org/wiki/Morgen!_(Richard_Strauss). Accessed 25 March 2010. It sounds better in the original German, and better still with the music attached.

Translated into explanatory English, her approach to her lover sounds as follows:

> KATERINA:
> Seryozha! My dearest!
> *(She snuggles up to Sergey. Sergey maintains a sullen silence)*
> At last!
> I've gone the whole day without seeing you
> Seryozha![15]

Translated into music, the same passage is transformed into a melting flow of melody, the words of the Russian libretto being sustained by their own translation into the sign system of music, which greatly intensifies their meaning and emotional impact. Even if sung in English, much of the impact would still be preserved through the musical embodiment of the words, although they might not fit the notes so snugly. Whereas in terms of the order of writing and purely denotative meaning one may take the words as being primary, and the music secondary, the effect in performance is exactly the opposite: we hear the music as pure emotion, logically preceding the words into which it is poured. And the musical phrase in question took on, sadly, a denotative life of its own, carrying layers of meaning which no longer depend on the original words. The same musical sequence from the scene in *Lady Macbeth* just quoted reappears many years later, in Shostakovich's eighth string quartet, completed in 1960. David Fanning quotes the original in his monograph on that quartet:[16]

15 Galina Vishnevskaya and others, Ambrosian Opera Chorus and London Philharmonic Orchestra perf. *Lady Macbeth of Mtsensk*. Conducted by Mstislav Rostropovich. By Dmitri Shostakovich. London, EMI Records, 1990. Accompanying booklet by Dmitri Shostakovich and Alexander Preis, librettists. Transliteration and trans. by Joan Pemberton Smith, 128–9.

16 David Fanning, *Shostakovich: String Quartet No. 8* (Burlington, Vermont and Aldershot: Ashgate, 2004), 117. Professor Fanning draws attention to other echoes of the 1934 opera within the 1960 quartet: see pp. 77, 115–20, 125.

b)

[Seryozha, my dearest! At last! I have not seen you all day, Seryozha.]

Shostakovich, Quartet No. 8, measures 479–85.

This time, the sequence refers not only to the sufferings of a provincial lady, but also to the sorrowful memories of the composer, whose career and even his life were threatened by the official disapproval that had suddenly overwhelmed his great opera, twenty-four years previously. The initial response of the critics had been hugely positive, and the work had gone through dozens of sold-out performances, until Stalin, as a man of culture, took it into his head to visit the show. His tastes offended, he left in disgust, and an editorial in *Pravda* denounced the 'crashing, gnashing and screeching' of the opera, which promptly disappeared for more than two decades, during which the composer lived under constant threat of abduction and murder by the police; the unsigned *Pravda* editorial, having criticized the composer's compositional procedures, had ended with an unmistakable threat: 'This is playing at abstruse things, which could end very badly'.[17]

The poignant beauty of a particular melody in the quartet's fourth movement thus recalls both his colossal artistic achievement and his downfall. Once the listener is told of the connection, the emotional impact of the passage in the Eighth Quartet is inevitably increased. The composer highlights his own presence in the quartet, as in many other works, by introducing and punctuating it with his musical signature, D-S-C-H. We are left in little doubt that the principal link between various quoted musical motifs in the work is their relevance to the composer's own emotional life and biography.

With this last example of the migration of a musical motif, we have moved outside the world of verbal texts in the strict sense. Meanings and emotions continue to invade even musical texts through associations. Things that we know, or think we know, about the genre, the composer, even the performer will influence our perception of music. Within the world of folk music, the marvelous Klezmer tradition gains multiple layers of emotional complexity because of the terrible fate of Central Europe's Jews, because of its relationship to non-Jewish Eastern European folk music, because its *home* language is Yiddish, because it has been preserved and revived following the mass murder of most of its original exponents, and for some people, perhaps, because it preserves an honourable Jewish cultural identity distinct from the currently dominant Israeli version. If one then listens to Itzhak Perlman, the Israeli-American violinist, performing the stately

17 See Solomon Volkov's Introduction to *Testimony: The Memoirs of Dmitri Shostakovich as related to and edited by Solomon Volkov*, trans. Antonina W. Bouis (London: Faber, 1981), xxix; see also Volkov's introductory note, 'The return of Lady Macbeth', in the booklet accompanying the 1990 digital re-issue of the 1979 EMI recording (note 15 above). Volkov's presentation of Shostakovich's life and views has sometimes been impugned, but on this point his account agrees with a broader consensus. Laurel Fay vividly renders *Pravda*'s puerile insults against the opera: 'Snatches of melody, embryos of a musical phrase drown, struggle free and disappear again in the din, the grinding, the squealing. ... The music quacks, hoots, pants, and gasps'. In *Shostakovich: A Life* (New York: Oxford University Press, 2000), 84–5.

dance 'Firn Di Mekhutonim Aheim' (Escorting the Parents of the Bride and Groom Home), composed by Naftule Brandwein, a clarinettist who emigrated to America and thereby escaped the Holocaust, an extra layer of emotional complexity may be added by the biographical detail that this music was played at the wedding of Perlman's own daughter.[18]

Music already has a direct line to the emotions, and can carry additional emotional freight by association with non-musical facts which then seem to be embodied in the sound – just as timbre and intonation, the rise of pitch and emotion, underpin the magnificent rhetoric of Martin Luther King, which requires an audio recording to experience, musically, his thrilling message of liberation. The impact is less on the printed page, and translation could scarcely hope to do it justice. It demands performance, and an audience that knows how to respond in chorus. Sound precedes sense in our apprehension of it.

> I have a dream that one day this nation will rise up and live out the true meaning of its creed: 'We hold these truths to be self-evident: that all men are created equal'. I have a dream that one day on the red hills of Georgia the sons of former slaves and the sons of former slave owners will be able to sit down together at the table of brotherhood. I have a dream that one day even the state of Mississippi, a desert state, sweltering with the heat of injustice, sweltering with the heat of oppression, will be transformed into an oasis of freedom and justice. I have a dream that my four little children will one day live in a nation where they will not be judged by the colour of their skin but by the content of their character. I have a dream today.[19]

18 Naftule Brandwein and Abe Schwartz Orchestra perf. *Klezmer!: Jewish Music From Old World To Our World*. Produced by Henry Sapoznik. Newton New Jersey, Shanachie Entertainment, 2000. Itzhak Perlman and Klezmer Conservatory Band perf. *Itzhak Perlman in the Fiddler's House*. New York, Angel Records 1995. Reissued in *Perlman plays Klezmer*. London, EMI Classics, 2006. [2 CDs plus video of the wedding in question].

19 From Martin Luther King Jr, Speech at the Lincoln Memorial, 28 August 1963. The same extract, in a perfectly decent Italian version which appears, uncredited, on several websites, shows the level of translation loss: 'Io ho un sogno, che un giorno questa nazione si leverà in piedi e vivrà fino in fondo il senso delle sue convinzioni: noi riteniamo ovvia questa verità, che tutti gli uomini sono creati uguali. Io ho un sogno, che un giorno sulle rosse colline della Georgia i figli di coloro che un tempo

The naïve model of translation, consisting simply of a text in one language crossing some sort of language divide in order to fetch up as a text in another language, has long been superseded. For decades now, various translation scholars have pointed out that the process also involves translating across cultures, across times, across social and technical systems, and for particular reasons and purposes. We also know that texts exist in an extra-textual world of needs and wants which provide the start-point or the end-point to many translation processes: for example, a commercial translation which does not make its addressee wish, however fleetingly, to buy the product that the originator wishes to sell must be accounted a failure, in a transactional sense, however philologically accurate it may be. Similarly with an emotional text, a translation which moves from L1 to L2 but fails to move the recipient has not communicated the originator's need to elicit emotion E2 in response to emotion E1. Because of the loss of the audio channel, it would be doubly difficult for a written translation to catch Dr King's need to reach his listeners emotionally.

What is the correct stance for the translator or interpreter to adopt in relation to the emotional content that may be associated with the source text? There are various possible answers to that question; sometimes the choice is simplified by the provision of guidelines. Under the recent US administration of George W. Bush, hundreds of Muslim captives (some of them apparently random kidnap victims trafficked by criminal gangs) were housed in a prison camp at Guantánamo, Cuba, and subjected to endless interrogations, accompanied by occasional torture, verbal rudeness, or the enactment of trashy pornographic fantasies, in order to extract confessions of having waged war against the USA, or, failing that, of feeling as if they

---

furono schiavi e i figli di coloro che un tempo possedettero schiavi, sapranno sedere insieme al tavolo della fratellanza. Io ho un sogno, che un giorno perfino lo stato del Mississippi, uno stato colmo dell'arroganza dell'ingiustizia, colmo dell'arroganza dell'oppressione, si trasformerà in un'oasi di libertà e giustizia. Io ho un sogno, che i miei quattro figli piccoli vivranno un giorno in una nazione nella quale non saranno giudicati per il colore della loro pelle, ma per le qualità del loro carattere. Ho un sogno, oggi!' See http://www.english-zone.com/holidays/mlk-dreami.html. Accessed 26 March 2010.

might like to do so.[20] Their English-speaking interrogators required the services of interpreters, as many of the captives (who were not to be called 'prisoners' but 'detainees', just as hunger striking at Guantánamo had to be rechristened 'voluntary fasting') happened to be native speakers of other languages.[21] In a memoir, one of the Army interpreters, Sergeant Erik Saar, summed up the advice he received from a fellow linguist:

> I asked her if the linguists went through any sort of training for interrogations. 'No', she said, 'we just give them a short briefing when they arrive. There are three things they need to remember. First, they are never to question the interrogator. Two, they should always stay "in character". In other words, if the interrogator is leaning back in his chair and speaking softly, then the linguist should do the same. If the interrogator stands up and screams, the linguist should do the same. And three, they should do their best to translate word for word and not try to add what they think the interrogator is trying to say'. ... The drill was to go in and turn yourself into whatever interrogator you happened to be teamed with that night; come out, turn back into yourself, and don't talk to anyone about what had transpired inside.[22]

This was the prescribed role-play for interrogation sessions, where the representation of power relationships was more meaningful than the (largely futile) questions being put to the captives. For ordinary day-to-day interactions, as when prisoners needed to see a camp doctor, the rules were more relaxed and humane:

> On the cellblocks, often as not I just talked to a detainee myself and didn't have to directly translate anything. If I was the intermediary between a detainee and a medic, MP, or psych tech, I had to stay with the meaning of what was said but could put

20 Erik Saar and Viveca Novak, *Inside The Wire: A Military Intelligence Soldier's Eyewitness Account of Life at Guantánamo* (New York: Penguin Press, 2005), 226–8.

21 For the suppression of emotive language, see Tom Clonan, 'Inside Guantánamo', *Irish Times Weekend Review*, Saturday, 22 October 2005.

22 Saar and Novak, *Inside The Wire*, pp. 176–7. The meeting of cultures produced interesting translation problems, as Saar recalls (p. 219): 'Ben kicked a chair in front of the guy and yelled, "You are going to rot in this place, you terrorist motherfucker!" *Motherfucker* really doesn't translate into Arabic very well. As the linguist, I was left to come up with my own equivalent insult while staying in character and yelling as loud as Ben was. It was tricky. Is *son of a whore* as good as *motherfucker*?'.

> it in my own words. In interrogations, though, I had to channel the interrogator – precise words, tone of voice, mood, even physical motions – and sometimes that took quite a bit of doing.[23]

Not having a precise script when dealing with the captives' medical and administrative problems meant that the interpreter became an interlocutor, a mediator, a fellow human being. This in turn earned him the suspicion of the camp guards, who had not benefited from the insights of Translation Studies and favoured a radically simple standard of interaction:

> [T]he guards reserved a special loathing for linguists. They didn't trust us because only we could understand what the detainees were saying, and they tended to think of us as sympathizers, a term at Gitmo that included anyone who betrayed any signs of compassion or empathy for the captives, or talked to them a little too long. … They thought we should just get in and out of their cellblocks quickly, with as little said as possible. An MP who saw me laughing at a detainee's joke once glared at me and said, 'What the fuck is wrong with you; are you one of them detainee lovers?'[24]

Emotion, then, was to be channelled within narrow, artificial boundaries. To be fair to the guards, in certain settings – such as a prison camp – a deliberate capping of the emotional temperature can paradoxically help to safeguard minimum humanitarian standards.[25]

23 Saar and Novak, *Inside The Wire*, 176.
24 Saar and Novak, *Inside The Wire*, 73.
25 The camp is a place where immediate damage can be caused by cultural stereotyping and distorted power relations, and transmitting genuine emotion may be a dangerous course of action. The psychologist Bruno Bettelheim recounts how, when he suffered frostbite in Buchenwald concentration camp in 1938, he deliberately refrained from making emotional appeals, or advancing clever or 'cunning' arguments when seeking permission from an SS man to enter the camp clinic in order have the dead flesh cut off. Bruno Bettelheim, *The Informed Heart: The Human Condition in Modern Mass Society* (London, Thames and Hudson, 1961), 218 ff. 'I tried to be matter-of-fact, avoiding pleading, deference, or arrogance' (220). This was because the delusional system of anti-semitism to which the SS subscribed claims that Jews are not only 'sneaky, sly, underhanded, and pushing … cowards and cheats who took advantage of Gentiles by deceitfulness' (227), but also members of a powerful international conspiracy bent on destroying everything the SS stood for. It was therefore vital to

In the free world outside of prison camps, emotional interaction generally tends to cement social relations in a positive way. Emotional bonding is particularly important to politicians, who must appeal simultaneously to contradictory constituencies – which may explain why Richard Nixon's speechwriter felt impelled to mimic the rhythms of Dr King's most famous speech, during the closing stages of Mr Nixon's acceptance address on 8 August 1968 at the Miami Beach Republican convention to nominate a candidate for President of the United States of America. There was a difference. Whereas the late Dr King had had a dream, Mr Nixon saw a day:

> I see a day when Americans are once again proud of their flag. ... I see a day when the President of the United States is respected and his office is honoured because it is worthy of respect and worthy of honour. ... I see a day when we can look back on massive breakthroughs in solving the problems of slums and pollution and traffic which are choking our cities to death. I see a day when our senior citizens and millions of others can plan for the future with the assurance that their government is not going to rob them of their savings by destroying the value of their dollars.[26]

The audio recording of this passage shows that the reference to the value of dollars evoked a ten-second wave of spontaneous applause from convention delegates. Behind the copied rhythms of the anaphora is an unspoken claim that Mr Nixon's pedestrian vision (which he delivers with dogged dullness) might share something of the stature and generosity of Dr King, who had been murdered in April of that year. The passage written for Mr Nixon was unsuited to its speaker, whose talents lay elsewhere. The rhythms of Dr King's appeal proved untranslatable into the world of Nixonian reassurance.

---

suppress any element of behaviour which might activate this supremely threatening, delusional figure in the camp guard's mind. Bettelheim got the medical treatment he needed, partly no doubt because of random luck (if one may speak of luck in such a setting), but also because he realized that 'most one-to-one interactions between prisoner and SS resulted only in a clashing of stereotypes', precluding 'any real interaction as between real persons' (230).

26 John T. Woolley and Gerhard Peters, The American Presidency Project [online]. Santa Barbara, CA. Available at: http://www.presidency.ucsb.edu/ws/?pid=25968. Accessed 26 March 2010. The same site offers a live audio recording of Nixon's acceptance speech at: http://www.presidency.ucsb.edu/medialist.php?presid=37.

More insidious than the false claim of emotional engagement may be the suppression of emotion that is seen as inappropriate, sometimes through adaptation, sometimes through old-fashioned translation with added censorship. The sanitizing of embarrassing emotions may be done for admirable motives, but (apart from being false and fraudulent) such a falsification of the record can also serve as part of a consensus of bad faith, which sets out to normalize one group of people, reputed to be essentially peace-loving and harmless, while demonizing another, reputed to have an unstoppable drive towards atrocity. In real life, all cultures are prone to evil actions, and we had better remember it.

The last major example I wish to cite comes from the extraordinarily emotional Psalm 157 (which I will quote in the King James Version), written in a time of enslavement when the very identity of the Hebrews was threatened with destruction. Psalm 157 starts with an enormously moving lament for misfortune, and ends with an enthusiastic endorsement of genocide: the deliberate destruction of the next generation of the enemy population.

> By the rivers of Babylon, there we sat down, yea, we wept, when we remembered Zion.
> We hanged our harps upon the willows in the midst thereof.
> For there they that carried us away captive required of us a song; and they that wasted us required of us mirth, saying, Sing us one of the songs of Zion.
> How shall we sing the Lord's song in a strange land?
> If I forget thee, O Jerusalem, let my right hand forget her cunning.
> If I do not remember thee, let my tongue cleave to the roof of my mouth; if I prefer not Jerusalem above my chief joy.
> Remember, O Lord, the children of Edom in the day of Jerusalem; who said, Rase it, rase it, even to the foundation thereof.
> O daughter of Babylon, who art to be destroyed; happy shall he be, that rewardeth thee as thou hast served us.
> Happy shall he be, that taketh and dasheth thy little ones against the stones.

The widest exposure this text has received in recent popular culture was Boney M's 1978 recording of a song titled 'By the rivers of Babylon' and based on the Psalm in question. This disco version, powerfully and emotionally sung by four Caribbean women, quotes extensively from the first four lines of Psalm 137 (King James Version), but then skips the rest of the Psalm, including its ending which cries out for a literally genocidal revenge on the perpetrators of the Hebrews' exile. Instead, the Boney M version inserts the end of Psalm 19 (verse 14) which prays 'Let the words of my mouth and the meditation of my heart, be acceptable in Your sight, O Lord' – admirable sentiments at which no liberal pluralist could plausibly take offence. This is an understandable artistic and creative response, especially if taken on behalf of a popular singing group which cannot risk losing its audience: their listeners might begin to feel less dancey if urged to kill an unspecified number of little children by smashing their skulls.

Some Christian translations of the Bible, serving specific population groups, opt for similar adaptations. The 1998 version by Mark Graham, from his 'Music for the Church of God', warns Babylon that its destruction is coming, and wishes happiness for the man who repays the Babylonians for all the things they have done to the Hebrews. In particular, Graham's version says, 'We will never forget about the children'.[27] To a casual reader, this detail sounds like a very understandable lament for one's own children who have been lost. To the informed reader, however, it is a specific resolution to annihilate one's enemies' children. It would be hard to imagine a better example of apparent innocence combined with murderous intent. Slightly less misleading, and less sinister, is the retaliation promised by the authors of the Easy English version:

> Lord, remember the people of Edom.
> This is what they said in the Day of Jerusalem.
> 'Knock it down, knock it down to its foundations!'
> Daughter of Babylon, someone will destroy you!
> That person will do to you what you did to us.
> He will be very happy then!
> He will catch your children and hit them with a rock.
> He will be very happy then![28]

27 Copyright Mark Graham, 1998. See http://cgmusic.org/cghymnal/graham/bytheriversofbabylon.htm. Accessed 26 March 2010.

28 See http://www.easyenglish.info/psalms/psalm137-taw.htm. Accessed 26 March 2010.

Here at least it is clear whose children are to be targeted, but the threat, and the emotion of destructive hatred that underpins it, is attenuated. Although the King James version promises a lethal assault on the Babylonian children, merely being 'hit' with a rock would not necessarily be fatal. Something hateful and murderous is made to look no worse than a harsh but reasonable punishment. Another strategy of normalization is to state candidly what is proposed, but in calm, objective language. A helpful, and neutral-sounding, explanatory note is provided by those unemotional scholars over at the New American Bible: 'Happy those who seize your children and smash them against a rock: the infants represent the future generations, and so must be destroyed if the enemy is truly to be eradicated'.[29]

By such devices – omission, distortion, obfuscation, bland explanation – the Bible is made to sound like a normal book conforming to present standards of decency and human rights. This is not always the case, and well-meaning attempts to conceal its darker emotions have considerable drawbacks. We are better off knowing the truth about what it is we are reading. Well-meaning concealment or bland glossing is not always an acceptable translation policy.

The truth is that many artistic and religious texts are riddled with emotional elements, some of them highly questionable, and all of them detracting from the pure detached contemplation of what we are reading. It may be true that the appreciation of art is, at its best, a kind of purified aesthetic appreciation, and that 'tears and laughter are, aesthetically, frauds'.[30] But these are frauds that many verbal artists work damned hard to perpetrate, and which translators have, in most cases, a moral duty to preserve, replicate and transmit.

29 *New American Bible* (Washington, DC: Confraternity of Christian Doctrine, 1970, 1986, 1991). See http://www.usccb.org/nab/bible/psalms/psalm137.htm. Accessed 26 March 2010.

30 José Ortega y Gasset, 'Notes on the Novel', in *The dehumanization of art, and other writings on art and culture*, trans. Willard R. Trask (Garden City, N.Y.: Doubleday, 1956). Quoted in Wayne C. Booth, *The Rhetoric of Fiction* (Chicago: University of Chicago Press, 1968), 119–20.

KATHLEEN SHIELDS

Auditory Images as Sites of Emotion: Translating Gerard Manley Hopkins into French

In this essay I make a case for the importance of auditory images as initiators and carriers of meaning in translation. Such images are part of the inescapable differences between languages and cultures that are inevitably encountered in the translation process. However, in the discipline of translation studies and in translation practice itself these images are often ignored in the interests of cognitive content which is regarded as the transfer of ideas as opposed to feelings. For instance, an obvious challenge to translators is the use of puns in the source text and an obvious solution is to quietly ignore such puns. Further on we shall see an example of this where a translator ignores puns in an ostensibly neutral scientific text in favour of a blander, abstracted meaning. Taking the example of one particularly challenging writer, Gerard Manley Hopkins, I propose to explore the two following questions. How has the matter of auditory imagery in translations been treated to date? How could it be incorporated more fully and usefully into translation studies now?

Within the confines of poetic and literary translation, attention is given to auditory images but, for reasons explored here, translators and critics are often awed by the formal properties of whole languages and the prestige of the original author. The consequence of this is that poetic translations can be viewed as being either highly wrought formal equivalents or flat cribs intended purely for decoding purposes. To suggest another way of approaching auditory images I take the challenges posed by translating Hopkins into French. Among translations of Hopkins, Pierre Leyris tends to the highly wrought end of the spectrum while Jean-Georges Ritz tends towards the crib.[1] The work of one particular translator, Bruno Gaurier, is an interesting case, as he is not afraid to mediate between auditory imagery and logical meaning, even to extrapolate from sounds in order to create a new layer of argument that adds to and comments upon the original. I consider this point in conjunction with the work of some translation scholars who have studied the relation of auditory, and other, images to meaning in translation in order to suggest ways in which attention to such imagery could be incorporated into contemporary translation studies.

Auditory imagery and meaning

The term auditory imagery takes us away from the literary critical use of prosody (phonetics and rhythm specific to one language or writer) and conveys the idea of the musical and kinaesthetic aspects of language use as they work to create meaning in the performance that is the translation. The term prosody conjures up another era, pre-dating translation studies and the 1960s. For literary critics prosody is rhythm and sound texture. For linguists, prosody combines variables such as stress, intonation, quantity and pauses in speech that concern units greater than the individual phonemes. In addition prosody includes tempo and rhythm.[2] In itself prosody is a worthy subject, yet it is not always useful in the study of translations because it either considers whole languages and literary traditions in isolation,

1 See Phyllis Gaffney, '"The achieve of, the mastery of the thing!": Pierre Leyris's verse translations of Gerard Manley Hopkins', in *The Practices of Literary Translation: Constraints and Creativity*, ed. Jean Boase-Beier and Michael Holman (Manchester: St Jerome, 1998), 45–58. I am indebted to this article for its account of Leyris as translator. It is also a more detailed study of Hopkins in French than I offer here. For this reason I have chosen to focus on a recent translator of Hopkins, Bruno Gaurier, not covered by the article.

2 Hadumod Bussmann, *Routledge Dictionary of Language and Linguistics*, trans. Gregory Trauth and Kerstin Kazzazi (London: Routledge, 1996), 389.

or else individual speech utterances in one language. Indeed, the literary critical approaches to prosody, deriving from Romantic conceptions, may partly explain the neglect of phonological and acoustic side of language in translation studies. Auditory imagery tends to be corralled off into formalist approaches to literary translation, because it is inescapable there.

The phonetic aspect, or the sound texture, appeals to the musical intelligence of the listener. Studies of translation in the Russian formalist tradition, such as that by Ephim Etkind, have devoted attention to the functions of alliteration, assonance, and startling patterns of meaning and sound combined.[3] The rhythmical aspect, with its implications for syntax and breathing, calls into play the kinaesthetic intelligence. Clive Scott, in his book on translating Baudelaire, has a lot of interesting things to say about the differences of rhythm between English and French, and the consequent amount of freedom the translator has, depending on 'the degree of the reader's rhythmic tolerance and adaptability'. How far can 'alternative rhythmic versions of a language be explored, in comfort, while apparently disregarding that language's "natural" prosody?'.[4] Etkind and Scott make good points about the process of translating auditory imagery from one language to another as one text relates to another. However, it is my intention here to broaden the scope of their approaches to include the social and historical moment of the translation.

Auditory imagery brings to the fore the inevitability of the whole process of recreating something radically different in the new language. It draws on the irrational, emotional, ludic and arbitrary parts of a language, the parts that cannot be easily isolated into logical semantic content. The term 'semantic content' itself requires definition: it need not be limited to rational meaning but ought also to encompass emotional meaning. The translating of auditory images mobilizes powerful individual and collective images, beliefs and values. It inevitably draws us – the translator and the reader – towards a new semantic content that is strongly, physically and

3 Ephim Etkind, *Un Art en crise: Essai de poétique de la traduction poétique* (Lausanne: L'Âge d'Homme, 1982).

4 Clive Scott, *Translating Baudelaire* (Exeter: University of Exeter Press, 2000), 29.

half-consciously embedded in compellingly different sounds. It raises the larger question of meaning in translation. What components of meaning need to be translated and how are these to be recreated in the process of translating? Different translators have different approaches to the question of semantic content and what aspects of the other language they should be translating. Like other human beings, translators have different learning styles, not necessarily limited to the linguistic intelligence alone.[5] Yet, however different individual translators may be, logical abstracted meaning dominates thinking about translation in the west. The consequence is that hermeneutic, linguistic, or pedagogical approaches often overlook acoustic information carried in texts.

While it is certainly true that the history of western translation theory, as Douglas Robinson points out, 'is at once far more complex and diverse and far more dialogically intertwined than is commonly thought'[6] it is nevertheless the case that a vital strand running through it is Bible translation and the importance of the authority of the ideas in the text to be translated. As André Lefevere comments, it is possible 'that the West has paid so much attention to translation because its central text, the Bible, was written in a language it could not readily understand, so that it was forced to rely on translators to legitimize power'.[7] A consequence of the importance of Bible translation was the idea that thought content was what was to be translated. As Lefevere argues elsewhere, up to 1800, 'language was considered a vehicle for the exchange of thought'.[8]

The idea that language is only a vehicle for the exchange of thought and its corollary, the separation of sound from sense, does not however disappear with the arrival of Schleiermacher and Hölderlin. It has been

5 Howard Gardner, *Frames of Mind: The Theory of Multiple Intelligences* (London: Heineman, 1983).

6 Douglas Robinson, *Western Translation Theory from Herodotus to Nietzsche* (Manchester: St Jerome, 2002), xx.

7 André Lefevere, *Translation/History/Culture: A Sourcebook* (London: Routledge, 1992), 3.

8 André Lefevere, 'Translation: Its Genealogy in the West', in *Translation, History & Culture*, ed. Susan Bassnett and André Lefevere (London: Cassell, 1990), 17.

pointed out that the multiplication of the number of translations in the west through the nineteenth century did not lead to parallel developments on a theoretical level, Germany excepted. [9] Andrew Chesterman's concept of memes in translation studies is a helpful one because it explains how powerful and even mutually contradictory ideas about translation can compete and coexist at the same historical moment.[10] Even after the German Romantics' radical approach to translation as the place where whole cultures are in contact, after structuralism and deconstruction, the idea that translations exist only to convey thought is very much alive and well in models of semantic transfer.

There are three studies that usefully challenge this dominant way of thinking. Douglas Robinson in his book *The Translator's Turn* makes a plea for the translator's subjectivity and the whole 'limbic' side of language use to be taken into account.[11] He argues that many western ideas about meaning are founded on biblical translation and on Augustinian dualist ideas about language.[12] The text to be translated can be separated into spirit (meaning or ideas) and into matter (all the rest which falls away or gets lost in translation). So, for example, to focus on translating the sound elements of a text feels 'counterintuitive'.[13]

Developing Robinson's argument, we could say on the one hand that 'semantic content' can include visual imagery and clear analogies because these are seen to appeal to the rational or scientific intelligence. In both folk and specialist metaphysics the visual is associated with outerness and active concentration upon something in the world, while the auditory is

9 Henri Van Hoof, *Petite Histoire de la traduction en occident* (Louvain-la-Neuve: Cabay, 1986), 85.

10 Andrew Chesterman, *Memes of Translation: The Spread of Ideas in Translation Theory* (Amsterdam: Benjamins, 2000), 8–14.

11 Douglas Robinson, *The Translator's Turn* (Baltimore and London: Johns Hopkins University Press, 1991), x.

12 Robinson, *The Translator's Turn*, 38–50.

13 Robinson, *The Translator's Turn*, 143.

linked to innerness and to passivity.[14] However, this separation is artificial because, as Jonathan Rée puts it, 'the voice is the place where the inward subjectivity of individual spirits intersects with the social and historical reality of human languages'.[15] On the other hand, 'matter' can include sound texture, rhythm, puns, jokes, slips of the pen or the tongue, quirky personal and collective intertextual references such as song lyrics, slogans and children's rhymes. As we will see from the examples that follow a translator can either decide to include such matter, and to use it as a way in to the reasoning in a text, or else decide to ignore it.

Against the general background of dualist assumptions about meaning as Robinson outlines it, Henri Meschonnic also proposes that meaning in translation is an integral matter. He attacks, in characteristic polemical way, the approach of 'traductologie' or translation as science which studies the equivalence of a certain kind of information.[16] Meschonnic's argument is that meaning encompasses far more than communication of cognitive messages. As theorist, poet, and translator he has consistently seen rhythm as central to translating because it brings the body into language.[17] For instance, in his essay 'Alors la traduction chantera' he links rhythm to breathing in his translation of the Hebrew psalms.[18] Rhythm organizes the movement of *parole* in writing, *parole* being described, after Saussure but with more emphasis on context, as the individual performance of speech in a given historical moment and social situation.[19]

For Meschonnic a new way of conceiving translation as something more than transfer of some of the messages in the text is necessary because cultural contacts are changing through globalization and decolonization. 'Et la pensée du langage s'est transformée. Elle est passée de la *langue* (avec ses catégories – lexique, morphologie, syntaxe) au *discours*, au sujet agissant,

14 Jonathan Rée, *I See a Voice: Deafness, Language and the Senses, a Philosophical History* (New York: Metropolitan Books, 1999), 3, 37, 52, 59.

15 Rée, *I See a Voice*, 8.

16 Henri Meschonnic, *Poétique du traduire* (Paris: Verdier, 1999), 21–3.

17 Meschonnic, *Poétique du traduire*, 15, 97–111.

18 Meschonnic, *Poétique du traduire*, 142–59.

19 Meschonnic, *Poétique du traduire*, 56 and 24.

dialoguant, inscrit prosodiquement, rhythmiquement dans le langage, avec sa physique'.[20] To paraphrase, thinking about language has moved from *langue* (with its categories of lexis, morphology and syntax) to *discours*, to the subject as agent with his or her physical nature, in dialogue with others, inscribed prosodically and rhythmically in language.

Both *The Translator's Turn* and *Poétique du traduire* are evidence of the increasing attention throughout the 1990s that was paid to the person of the translator, as subjective practitioner, as historical agent and as cultural intermediary. These developments open up possibilities for more attention to be given to auditory imagery in translation. On the one hand the focus on the person of the translator allows us to study the part auditory images play in the creative process of translating. On the other hand the interest in translators as cultural intermediaries allows us to focus on auditory images as repositories of collective assumptions and lore.

A third study of how translators use auditory images in their work as cultural intermediaries presents these acoustic features as examples of the translator's unconscious. Lawrence Venuti approaches meaning by leaving to one side the overt messages of the translations and takes very seriously the mistakes of experienced translators, whether they interpolate intertextual layers from song lyrics or misconstrue false cognates. These mistakes communicate individual and collective beliefs and wishes and appear in the text as repressed meaning alongside the overt semantic content defined as 'lexicographical equivalence'.[21] Venuti shows translators unconsciously manipulating auditory images whether it is in order to express a pre-Babelian wish to transcend irreconcilable differences between languages, or to salve a liberal conscience, or to challenge the authority of the original author (p. 234).

Drawing on Freud and Lacan, Venuti distinguishes between the unconscious and what he calls the 'preconscious'. While the unconscious

20 Meschonnic, *Poétique du traduire*, 13.

21 Lawrence Venuti, 'The difference that translation makes: the translator's unconscious', in *Translation Studies: Perspectives on an Emerging Discipline*, ed. Alessandra Riccardi (Cambridge: Cambridge University Press: 2002), 237.

corresponds to repressed individual and collective beliefs and wishes, the preconscious is linked to translator strategies that are part of the learned tricks of the trade. These strategies are under conscious individual control but common to the whole profession and are encompassed by Gideon Toury's examples of behavioural norms among translators, 'the cultural and social norms that shape the translating process, especially the translating traditions, conventions, and practices that currently prevail in the receiving culture'.[22]

There is no doubt that the unconscious is important for translators in the same way as it is important for any creative work. The unconscious need not even be the site of repressed wishes but can also simply throw up creative solutions. Pierre Leyris, for example, describes how he once got stuck while translating a piece by Stephen Crane and how when he was half asleep his subconscious presented him with the right word.[23] However, what I would like to add to this picture is the idea that readers and translators also carry cultural baggage in their minds that is not necessarily unconscious, repressed or in conflict with the dominant cognitive meaning of a given text. Auditory images provide access to this storehouse of ideas that can lead to and even create logical and rational meaning.

The case of Hopkins in French

Umberto Eco, in a humorous but serious article on the arts of forgetting, points out that collective (or institutional) memory and its arts can be just as quirky and illogical as those of any individual. Because they are

22 Venuti, 'The Translator's Unconscious', 237.

23 Gaffney, '"The achieve of, the mastery of the thing!": Pierre Leyris's verse translations of Gerard Manley Hopkins', 58.

collective they seem normal.[24] This part of ourselves, not repressed, but half-remembered, half-forgotten that we take for granted, like so much unexamined junk in the attic, is what I term, further on in this essay, the pre-literate. It is a great resource, waiting to be pressed into service by the translator, sorted and used to reinforce a meaning or to create an ambiguity, to set up resonances or dissonances in the text.

To illustrate this point I take an extract from a recent French translation of 'The Wreck of the Deutschland', a long poem by Hopkins. The reason for this choice is firstly because Hopkins was himself as a writer very strongly attuned to auditory features of languages. Secondly, Hopkins presents an extreme challenge to translators into French and seems to attract them because he forces them to draw on different resources of meaning at their disposal. Bruno Gaurier is the latest in a long line of French translators to tackle Hopkins, Audigier and Gallet, Leyris, Mambrino, Ritz and Roditi.[25] His parallel text, *Gerard Manley Hopkins: Poèmes*, based on the Robert Bridges edition of 1918 with additions from the first collected edition of 1930, won the Prix Nelly Sachs in 2003, a prestigious translation prize established by the city of Dortmund in 1961.[26]

What follows is stanza four, printed facing the English version:

IV

[Sable je sasse
Au sablier – Dos au mur
Amarré, miné pourtant par une rafale, un tourbillon;
Et ce sont force voiles et déferlantes vers la chute;
Et moi sans mouvement, tel l'eau d'un puits, suspendu, transparent,
Mais en rappel toujours, chutant de toute la hauteur des
Murs, ou flancs de la montagne, nerf
De la profération évangélique, pression, principe, don du Christ.]

24 Umberto Eco, 'An *Ars Oblivionalis*? Forget It!', trans. Marilyn Migiel, *PMLA* 103.3 (May 1988), 254–61.

25 Gaffney, '"The achieve of, the mastery of the thing!": Pierre Leyris's verse translations of Gerard Manley Hopkins', 46.

26 Bruno Gaurier, trans., *Gerard Manley Hopkins: Poèmes* (Suilly-la-Tour: Le Décaèdre, 2003).

IV
I am soft sift
In an hourglass – at the wall
Fast, but mined with a motion, a drift,
And it crowds and it combs to a fall;
I steady as a water in a well, to a poise, to a pane,
But roped with, always, all the way down from the tall
Fells or flanks of the voel, a vein
Of the gospel proffer, a pressure, a principle, Christ's gift.[27]

Here Bruno Gaurier has done something wonderful with the sound patterns, reproducing some of the English sounds in French (such as the [s] of the sand in the first line and the [pr] in the last) and introducing others (such as the [a] and [y] sounds) throughout the stanza. In the fourth line he has consciously created an alternating pattern between unvoiced and voiced [f] and [v] to mimic the sound of storms blowing: '...et ce sont force voiles et déferlantes vers la chute'. But as he has informed me, sound and meaning are constantly cross-checked against each other during the process of translating.

In many instances the rational structure of an image is laid down by the sounds. Keeping the [s] sound in the first line ('I am soft sift/ In an hourglass' 'Sable je sasse/ au sablier') leads Gaurier to create a striking image in French that adds an extra layer of meaning. The alliteration on [s] gives rise to the image of the *sas*, which in the finished text shows up the outlines of the translation process. The noun *sas* can mean a sieve or a canal lock. It is a kind of intermediary space, such as the double security doors at a bank or an airport, where one person passes through at a time. The verb *sasser* is very rare but is normally used transitively with a direct object. Here the unusual intransitive use of it captures the sense of the individual pushing through time without acting on anything. The new image replicates the Hopkins hourglass and extrapolates from it, developing the metaphor, 'I am a grain of sand' even further.

Bruno Gaurier described in correspondence how the image came to him suddenly as he was waiting at airport security gates.

27 Gaurier, *Gerard Manley Hopkins: Poèmes*, 31 and 30.

> La question du sas: … c'est le terme employé pour le passage entre les deux doubles portes des bâtiments publics, ou bien quand on parle de ce passage entre la navette Discovery et l'unité qui se trouve en orbite, à laquelle la navette doit se raccrocher: pour passer de l'une à l'autre. … Je pense aussi au chas d'une aiguille (eye of a needle), par lequel ne peut 'sasser' (j'ai inventé dans ce néologisme le passage du substantif au verbe conjugé) le riche, pas plus qu'un chameau.
> [About the *sas*: … it's the term used for the space between the two double doors in public buildings, or else when you are referring to the passage between the Discovery shuttle and the unit which is in orbit, which the shuttle has to join to: to pass from one to the other … I'm also thinking of the eye of a needle, through which (I've invented with this neologism a passage from the substantive to the conjugated verb) the rich man cannot *sass*, no more than a camel.][28]

The analogy between the sand in the hourglass and waiting inside security gates is one that summons up a common experience of travellers in the early twenty-first century: there is the idea of a difficult passage because one is waiting, wondering when one can pass through the narrow space. Where does the image come from? Not from any unconscious motives. Rather the [s] sounds lead the writer to make subjective links, but these links are also collective and shared.

Auditory imagery reminds us of the oral qualities of language, that is to say its non-literate aspects. More importantly it draws us into the realm of what the poet Seamus Heaney calls the 'pre-literate'.[29] Speaking of the subculture of sectarian rhymes and childhood experience growing up in Northern Ireland, Heaney says, 'the sub-cultures … are not altogether a subculture in that they aren't forgotten about. They are the basis of many people's pieties, perhaps'.[30] At the risk of multiplying categories, I would like to bring this third element of the pre-literate to the preconscious and the unconscious. The pre-literate differs from the unconscious in that it is half-remembered, not repressed. The pre-literate is at the points in the translator's subjectivity where collective literary practices meet the

28 B.G. in correspondence with K.S., 10 August 2005.

29 Seamus Heaney, *Preoccupations: Selected Prose 1968–1978* (London: Faber, 1980), 26.

30 Seamus Heaney, Interview with Eavan Boland on RTÉ Radio, 22 September 1970.

individual. Song-lyrics are a good example of the pre-literate, as they are often half-remembered and are not always an example of repression.

Summary: auditory imagery and meaning in the translation process

A: UNCONSCIOUS: repressed individual and collective beliefs and wishes (Venuti)
B: PRE-LITERATE: aural and oral, musical and kinaesthetic aspects of language, e.g. cultural baggage and collective meaning including rhymes, proverbs, songs, jokes, weather lore, jingles, song lyrics, political soundbites, advertising (Eco, Heaney)
C: PRECONSCIOUS: translator training, behavioural patterns (Toury), regular practices, institutional cultures, inculcation (Simeoni)
D: CONSCIOUS: translator notebooks, translators' conscious decisions, Think Aloud Protocols, Skopos theory (i.e. purpose of translation) (Chesterman)

It is during childhood language acquisition that the pre-literate elements of language, the musical and kinaesthetic, are absorbed. Hopkins was acutely attuned to them and, for example, explains that he developed his sprung rhythm from children's rhymes and from weather lore. The pre-literate aspects of language are also very clear when we encounter another language and start to acquire it as adults. For example, it was as an adult student and translator of Welsh that Hopkins developed the patterns of assonance that are to be found in his English poetry.[31] It is probably true to say that experienced translators have internalized their other language(s) to the extent that this awareness has become dulled over time. However, writers and translators tend to be more than averagely attuned to the importance of the meanings conveyed by the pre-literate.

31 Norman White, *Hopkins: A Literary Biography* (Oxford: Clarendon Press, 1992), 263.

Puns and poetry: avoidance or engagement

In translations, drawing on the pre-literate as a resource is often seen as evidence of the translator's subjectivity and as something to be avoided. But there are moments when translators are confronted head-on by the auditory qualities of the source text and must face or avoid the challenge of creatively drawing on their own pre-literate resources. A not infrequent case is when there are puns in the source text, and this can arise in neutral and scientific genres, not just in poetry, as the following example shows. In an academic paper on the future of French in a globalizing world, the linguist Robert Chaudenson makes three plays on words when he writes [my italics]:

> In 1989 I proposed three principal species of *Franco-fauna* (Chaudenson 1989):
>
> 1. People who can handle all language situations in French
> 2. Limited French speakers ('*Francophonoïdes*')
> 3. Very limited French speakers ('*Franco-aphones*').[32]

The meaning of the first pun is conveyed but the auditory element in *francophone* and *franco-faune* is perhaps inevitably hard to catch in English. Perhaps 'French-speaking fauna' would convey more of the meaning? The translator has refrained from trying to do anything with the pseudo-scientific suffix *-oïdes* but could have given something like 'Francophonoids' in English in the second case. In the third pun the idea of 'mute' or 'silent' which is conveyed by the last pun on the suffix '*-aphones*' could be rendered by something like 'Francomutes'.

The translator is not shying away from the authority of the author's subjectivity because the French puns are presented as they occurred in the

32 Robert Chaudenson, 'Geolinguistics, geopolitics, geostrategy: the case of French' in *Languages in a Globalizing World*, ed. Jacques Maurais and Michael A. Morris (Cambridge: Cambridge University Press, 2003), 291–7 (p. 293).

original. It is more the case that the translator is reluctant to delve into his or her own subjectivity to deal with the acoustic intertextuality of the source text, thereby losing a rhetorical resource. Robert Chaudenson, a linguist who has published widely on creole languages, by making these puns, is undermining the aspirational nature of the statistics on *francophonie*. In the rest of his article he questions the accuracy of statistics given by government bodies of French-speaking countries when they break speakers into categories and he puns in order to back up his questioning of the statistics. The translator respects the both the neutral tone of the scientific academic paper and the reputation of the author too much to make anything of the puns in English. Translator training warns us not to be too creative with the source text. In this case the ludic would disturb the neutral scientific tone of the linguist as expert. The acoustic information present in texts is both subjective and collective. Yet it is often the case that translators who are trained to convey rational semantic content are afraid to develop the acoustic information held in the text for fear of putting their own subjectivity in evidence.

In their practice literary translators have something useful to teach in this regard. Rather than becoming vexed by the question of whether the translation as a product is a tour de force or a failure, when confronted by prosodic elements they become engaged with the processes of navigating between meaning and sound. It is impossible to operate a separation between semantic content on the one hand and acoustic meaning on the other. For example, in the process of translating the Hopkins poem, 'Spring and Fall' it is not a case of pouring meaning into a mould of octosyllables.

The French translators try to reactivate the sound and meaning patterns in line 8 of 'Spring and Fall': 'Through worlds of wanwood leafmeal lie'. The line is at a symmetrical point, exactly half way through the poem, so that the sounds and images hark back to the beginning with its falling leaves, and to the last line with its evocation of death and mourning for the passing of one's own life. In line 8 'leafmeal' points forward to the decay, the 'blight' at the end. Both the Leyris and Gaurier translations bring out this symmetry, Leyris with, 'Un monde effeuillé de bois mort' and Gaurier with the more explicit, 'Quand gisent exsangues des tas de bois dans les ramées éparses'. They have not ignored the acoustic information in the text but have extrapolated from it and made the logical meaning explicit.[33]

The Hopkins compounds, 'wanwood' and 'leafmeal' are hard to do in French. To translate them with the noun+de+noun beloved of surrealist writers would run the risk of syntactical monotony with 'de' being repeated too many times. The French translators have either attenuated or dropped the sound patterning in favour of keeping the symmetry in meaning, a meaning that has nevertheless been created by the sounds. As Clive Scott says, 'translation ... is committed to sustaining the openness, the unfinishedness in time and across national boundaries, of the source text.[34] The semantic symmetries of 'Spring and Fall' are lost on the English speaker who is bowled over by the sound patterns of 'wanwood' and 'leafmeal' at the expense of the ideas of human death and decay that they convey. The French translations bring us back to the symmetry of meaning integral to the sounds.

From the 1960s onwards translation studies grew out of literary criticism on the one hand and out of linguistics on the other. From literary criticism it drew on formalism and on hermeneutics, hence the emphasis on the function, status and interpretation of translated texts and the proliferation of metaphors for describing these. As a form of literary criticism it tended to link auditory images either to whole languages or to brilliant individual solutions. As a discipline translation studies has yet to incorporate both the subjective and collective sides to auditory imagery. At the moment the very term prosody seems old-fashioned and hard to relate to current theories. One explanation for this is that traditional approaches to prosody tend to focus on contrasts between whole languages, each language seen as having its own irreducible musical and rhythmical differences. To take the case of Hopkins as an example, French translators will inevitably encounter the idea that French can't do 'sprung rhythm' because with sprung rhythm what counts is stress and extra unstressed syllables

33 See Gaffney for a full discussion of this poem and translations.

34 Scott, *Translating Baudelaire*, 29.

can be disregarded. French poetry, song and speech are syllabic with tonic accents where every syllable counts. The overall effect on the listener is one of smoothness compared with English. This is why contemporary French music tends to prefer reggae and rap to rock and roll (though of course there are significant counter-examples of French rock). However, to view languages and translations in this way is to focus on them as products, rather than as examples of different types of process.

For Bruno Gaurier the tonic accents in French can be used to create the ebb and flow of a musical wave, like plain chant, so as to recreate the effect of sprung rhythm in English. The translator needs to have some linguistic sentiment for the languages and to straddle the rhythmical systems of both in order to compose the translation.

> Je suis très attaché aux accents toniques, à tout ce qui fait le rythme, car dans le rythme ... se trouve une large part du sens. ... Certains disent que la langue française est inaccentuée. Ce n'est pas juste: elle comporte un certain génie des accents, et traduire depuis l'anglais requiert précisément de bien connaître les insondables ressources et ressorts de notre propre langue française. En celà, pour bien traduire, il faut être amoureux des deux langues, composer dans les deux langues.[35]
> [I am very attached to the tonic accents and to everything that creates rhythm, for in rhythm ... lies a large part of the meaning ... Some say that the French language is unaccentuated. This is not right: French has its own way with accents, and translating from English requires a knowledge of the unfathomable depths and springs of our own French language. For that, to translate well you must be in love with the two languages, compose in the two languages.]

Considerations of prosody end up recycling some familiar and well-worn eighteenth-century and Romantic claims about languages and translation, for instance, the idea that languages can be classified typologically according to their 'genius'. The characteristic prosody of whole languages is an offshoot of this idea which undoubtedly has its truth but which does not tell us enough about the reality of translating auditory imagery. Romantic ideas about languages live on in literary criticism so that when it comes to the meanings conveyed by the sound elements of a language, individual

35 B.G. in correspondence with K.S., 2005.

translations are often read as instances of rare brilliance. Creative solutions for sound effects are seen to arise from the genius of the author (and very occasionally from the genius of the translator). Yet in practice the translator's subjectivity cannot work with the idea of one language and its genius or with the idea that creativity is impossible.

Auditory images and translation studies

From linguistics, from the 1960s onwards, translation studies sought to elaborate scientific models. The discipline of linguistics has itself been criticized from within for its exclusive focus on the rational and its refusal to engage with the question of emotion when dealing with issues such as language loyalty, bilingualism and code switching. For instance, Rajagopalan argues that:

> an important part of the reason why we linguists have traditionally had little or no appreciable success in influencing public opinion with respect to language, let alone having a say in language planning and state policies, is that we have by and large tended to overlook or downplay the emotional aspect of language. Instead, the human linguistic faculty is typically viewed as an attribute of the reasoning mind. In other words, it is believed that man is *homo loquens* because, unlike any of the other, lower order species in the animal kingdom, he is *homo sapiens*. On the other hand, as far as the person on the street is concerned, the language issue is full of emotional connotations.[36]

Even sociolinguistics is not exempt from classifying itself as a hard, rational science and from distancing itself from the thoughts and emotions of language users. It has been taken to task for emptying itself of the sociology of language, that is the study of problems of society as they correlate to language use, in favour of statistical and quantitative models that do not

36 Kanavillil Rajagopalan, 'Emotion and Language Politics: The Brazilian Case', *Journal of Multilingual and Multicultural Development*, 25, 2–3 (2004), 105–23 (108).

account for language change.[37] From linguistics translation studies has inherited this suspicion of emotion and the idea that semantic content equates to rational meaning.

This was why the descriptive approach to translation studies in the work of Toury, Lambert, Hermans and others was such a breath of fresh air when it appeared in the mid-1970s. Accepting translations as they are received into the target culture frees the translator (and the translation reader and user) from the double bind of extreme effacement before the genius of a language and individual strokes of fortuitous artistic brilliance. There is room for approaches to auditory imagery in the description of the function of translations within the receiving target-language system(s). One of the legacies of descriptive translation studies is that translating is now seen as process of production and reception involving different interacting systems: literary, media, political, cultural, educational, etc. Prosody still carries with it the outmoded idea of translation as product yet there is no reason why the auditory qualities of a translation cannot be incorporated into the idea of translation as process.

Andrew Chesterman has distinguished three major groupings in contemporary translation studies depending on whether it is viewed as a humanistic discipline, as an applied science (translator training comes in here) or as a human science like psychology or sociology.[38] These three strands are increasingly exerting an influence on each other. From about the 1980s onwards translation studies took a 'cultural turn' corresponding to the equivalent 'linguistic turn' taking place in historical studies so that translations came more and more to be considered as points where cultures were in contact. From the 1990s the focus of attention has been on the person of the translator. From 2000 this interest in the translator has continued but with an emphasis on the translator in society. It may be that the field is taking a 'sociological turn'.

37 Deborah Cameron, 'Demythologizing Sociolinguistics', in *Ideologies of Language*, ed. John E. Joseph and Talbot J. Taylor (London: Routledge, 1990), 79–93.

38 Andrew Chesterman, 'Semiotic Modalities in Translation Causality', *Across Languages and Cultures* 3.2 (2002), 145–58 (145–8).

These developments open up possibilities for more attention to be given to auditory imagery in translation: the cultural turn allows us to focus on auditory images as repositories of the pre-literate. The focus on the person of the translator allows us to study the importance of auditory images in the creative process of translating. The sociological turn could lead to studies of the part that auditory images play in drawing on the collective storehouse of meaning in the production and reception of translated texts. When we stand outside a language or a culture the pre-literate seems arbitrary or even weird, as with the example of Robert Chaudenson's puns. When we are within a culture and a language it is so obvious it tends to be dismissed, as Umberto Eco has said. Translations can shed new light on the obvious and on those parts of meaning that tend to be overlooked.

Auditory imagery occupies the pre-literate ground between the translator's own subjectivity and the collective. Musical and rhythmical meaning are not necessarily only to do with repressed desires but can connect directly to logical meaning, and even give rise to logical images as we have seen with the example of Bruno Gaurier's translation of 'The Wreck of the Deutschland'. In other words emotional meaning can be constitutive of rational meaning while the emotional elements of a text are also an important part of its meaning which should not be overlooked. A case in point is auditory imagery which can often reinforce rational argument without perforce contradicting or undermining it. Sound need not always be opposed to sense.

MICHAEL CRONIN

A Dash of the Foreign: The Mixed Emotions of Difference

Writing for *An Claidheamh Soluis* [The Sword of Light] in 1915, Tadhg Ó Donnchadha, a prominent translator of Welsh literature into Irish, had the following to say about the restorative virtue of translation:

> [It is a good thing, however, to look around us now and again, and to learn about the work being done in other languages. If we want Irish to flourish again, we must nourish it in the meantime with a dash of the foreign. New thoughts and new arts and new literary devices, those are what we need. It is things of that sort from foreign languages that will excite our own writers to emulate them. And if the foreign is a good thing, it is essential to be careful about it and to filter it clean before it is used.]
> Is maith an rud é, amh, féachaint timcheall orainn anois agus arís, agus eólus d'fhagháil ar an saothrú atá dhá dhéanamh i dteangthaibh eile. Má's mian linn athfhás do theacht ar an nGaedhilg ní mór dúinn í bheathú idir dhá linn ar steall don iasacht. Smaointe nua, agus ealadhna nua, agus 'giúirléidí' nua litridheachta, is iad atá i n-easnamh orainn. Solaiodí dá sórd a teangthaibh iasachta iseadh a ghríosóidh ár scríbhneoirí féin chun aithris ortha. Acht má's maith é an t-iasacht, ní mór bheith cúramach n-a thaobh agus é scagadh glan sara mbaintear feidhm as.[1]

Translation for Ó Donnchadha was a good thing but for the translator as cultural nationalist it was good only insofar as it subscribed to a teleology of purity. The contact with the foreign was welcome, on the condition that the appropriate filter was in place to thoroughly domesticate the threat of otherness. So in this partial and overdetermined view of language development and translation history, translation was always potentially a bearer of impurities, and one source of such impurity was a language that although

1 Cited in Philip O'Leary, *The Prose Literature of the Gaelic Revival* (Pennsylvania: Pennsylvania University Press, 1994), 391–2.

deemed 'foreign', was all too familiar, English. But there was English and there was English. When John Mitchel's *Jail Journal* was rendered into Irish, the anonymous reviewer in the publication *Sinn Féin* reviewing the translation remarked on the debate surrounding the translation of foreign literatures into Irish and claimed that the:

> Consensus of opinion would seem to indicate that modern Irish literature ought to include translations of the best works of those Anglo-Irish writers whose sympathies were national, and who had anything in them of what is called the Gaelic spirit.[2]

If it was the express wish of writers like Pádraig Pearse and Pádraic Ó Conaire that European languages other than English be the primary source of any material translated into Irish, when the new State came into being it was the 'consensus of opinion' which was to prevail and English became the primary source language for the State-sponsored translation project launched by An Gúm.[3] This did not mean the wholesale translation of writers like Yeats, O'Casey, Lady Gregory and Synge, however, into Irish, *pace* the *Sinn Féin* reviewer, but predominantly the translation of the middle-brow reading matter of Victorian and Edwardian England.[4]

What the theoreticians of the Gaelic revival brought to the fore was the inextricable link between the forging of a new cultural and linguistic identity and the question of translation. If the Irish had, in a sense, in the nineteenth century been translated into English and if they were to translate themselves back into Irish, then they would have to look at how translation was going to assist or hinder them in the task. In asking the question, they were not dissimilar to many other national groups in Europe and elsewhere who would look to translation as a way of both consolidating and elaborat-

2 Anon., 'New Irish Books', *Sinn Féin*, 10 June 1911, p. 6.

3 Michael Cronin, *Translating Ireland* (Cork: Cork University Press, 1996), 153–61. *An Gúm* was the publishing division of the Irish Department of Education whose aim was to promote literacy in the Irish language in the post-independence period.

4 See Philip O'Leary, *Gaelic Prose in the Irish Free State 1922–1939* (Dublin: UCD Press, 2004).

ing linguistic and cultural identity.[5] If material in translation was to be a resource for writers in Irish, it is fair to say that it was the condition of translation that was to be a resource for writers in English. In other words, the far-reaching effects of Douglas Hyde's translation work in the 1890s were less to do with the actual material that he brought into the English language from Irish than with the fact that he revealed to writers in English that the condition of being translated might reveal a strength as much as a defect. Declan Kiberd, in his study of Synge and the Irish language, noted the paradoxical outcome of Hyde's enterprise:

> The translation was included simply to help the student who found difficulty with the Irish, for the object of the work was to popularise the spread of Irish literature. It soon became clear, however, that the main appeal of the book [*The Love Songs of Connacht*] to Yeats and his contemporaries lay in Hyde's own translations, and especially in those translations written in Anglo-Irish prose rather than in verse. The very success of the book caused the defeat of its primary purpose. Instead of popularising Irish literature, it made the creation of an Irish literature in English seem all the more plausible.[6]

The question then of Hiberno-English is indissociable from the linguistic company it keeps in the form of Irish and from its structural dependence on the fact of that language in the way in which the specific lexical and syntactic resources of Hiberno-English came into being.[7] However, the relationship between Irish and Hiberno-English is not simply one of linguistic proximity and lexical and syntactic indebtedness. It is also, as Kiberd suggests, agonistic in the vying for cultural and political pre-eminence in the New Ireland. There was much at stake emotionally in which language

5 Pascale Casanova, *La République mondiale des lettres* (Paris: Seuil, 1999), 241–82 and 347–410.

6 Declan Kiberd, *Synge and the Irish Language*, 2nd edn (Dublin: Gill and Macmillan, 1993), 197.

7 Markku Filippula, *The Grammar of Irish English* (London: Routledge, 1999); T.P. Dolan, *A Dictionary of Hiberno-English: The Irish Use of English* (Dublin: Gill and Macmillan, 1998); Terence Dolan, 'Translating Irelands: the English Language in the Irish context', in *The Languages of Ireland*, ed. Michael Cronin and Cormac Ó Cuilleanáin (Dublin: Four Courts Press, 2003), 78–92.

would win out as the primary mode of national expression. What I would like to suggest in this essay is that if translation acted as the crucible for the emergence of a distinctive literature in Hiberno-English in Modern Ireland, translation is once more playing a role in the reconfiguration of the relationship between Irish and English in Late Modern Ireland. The reconfiguration is one that is altering the emotional terms of exchange between the two languages and points to a set of strategies that undermine some of the more conventional assumptions about the fraught relationship between language and politics in Ireland.

A significant episode in the history of translation in Ireland was the decision by a number of publishers such as Goldsmith Press, Raven Arts Press and Wolfhound Press in the 1980s to publish bilingual anthologies of contemporary Irish poetry.[8] The novelty lay in the fact that it was modern Irish poetry rather than ancient Irish texts which were being translated and that the translations were largely the work of writers rather than scholars. Though the policy was not without controversy, it established a pattern for the presentation and reception of a considerable body of modern poetry written in Irish which was henceforth accompanied by translations in English.[9] What about the English that we find in these translations? To what extent is the English foregrounded as being distinctively Irish? To what extent, in other words, is there a continuation or a repudiation of the Hydean dynamic, is the reader being made aware of the distinct otherness of Irish shadowing the translations or have the protocols of standardized English removed traces of language contact or difference? To answer these questions, the essay will examine collections of selected poems by two of the most prominent poets in modern Irish, Gabriel Rosenstock and Louis de Paor.

* * *

8 Dermot Bolger, ed., *An Tonn Gheal/ The Bright Wave* (Dublin: Raven Arts Press, 1986); Declan Kiberd and Gabriel Fitzmaurice, ed., *An Crann faoi Bhláth/ The Flowering Tree* (Dublin: Wolfhound Press, 1991); Douglas Sealy and Tomás Mac Siomóin, ed., *Máirtín Ó Direáin: Tacar Dánta/ Selected Poems* (Athlone: The Goldsmith Press, 1984).

9 For details on the controversy see Cronin, *Translating Ireland*, 174–9.

Gabriel Rosenstock, a member of *Aosdána*, was born in Co Limerick in 1949 and is one of the most prolific writers and translators in Irish with over one hundred titles to his name. He was closely associated with the journal *Innti* founded by Micheál Davitt in University College Cork in 1970 which had the aim of bringing the idiom of contemporary life into poetry in modern Irish. His first collection of selected poems *Rogha Rosenstock* was published in 1994 and his second selection was published as *Rogha Dánta* in 2005.[10] Louis de Paor, born in Cork in 1961, was also associated with *Innti* magazine although at a later stage. His collections include *Próca Solais is Luatha* [Urn of Light and Ashes] which won the won Duais an Ríordánaigh; *Aimsir Bhreicneach* [Freckled Weather], which was short-listed for the Victorian Premier's Award for Literary Translation and a collection of selected poems, *Ag Greadadh Bas sa Reilig* [Clapping in the Cemetery].[11]

Robert Welch in his presentation of the poetry of Rosenstock situates him both in a specific place and in a wider world. The specific place is University College Cork in the late 1960s and the wider world is the poet's frame of cultural and imaginative reference. Welch claims that 'Gabriel Rosenstock's poetry is world poetry' and that as a student Rosenstock was:

> Immersed in Freud, Nietzsche and Kant; the translations from the Chinese of Arthur Waley; Ezra Pound; the Dadaists and the Surrealists; and the poetry of Eoghan Rua Ó Súilleabháin, Aogán Ó Rathaille and Geoffrey Keating. He read the Tibetan *Book of the Dead*, studied magic, and there was an iron gleam in his eye that gave you to understand that he was dead serious about all of this.[12]

Part of Welch's contention is that Irish is as much a way out as a way in for Rosenstock. Challenging the exilic convention of a strain of Irish

10 Gabriel Rosenstock, *Rogha Rosenstock* (Indreabhán: Cló Iar-Chonnachta, 1994); Gabriel Rosenstock, *Rogha Dánta* (Indreabhán: Cló Iar-Chonnachta, 2005).

11 Louis de Paor, *Próca Solais is Luatha* (Dublin: Coiscéim, 1988); *Aimsir Bhreicneach* (Canberra: Leros Press, 1993); *Ag Greadadh Bas sa Reilig* (Indreabhán: Cló Iar-Chonnachta, 2005).

12 Robert Welch, 'The Bengal Tiger', in Gabriel Rosenstock, *Rogha Dánta*, v.

modernism where the only way to embrace the world was to repudiate the sod and undo the nets of piety, prudery and patria, Rosenstock's writing suggests another path where a complex and detailed immersion in Irish traditions brings him into contact with the literatures and cultures of elsewhere. Welch, for example, claims that in the poem 'Xolotl',

> Rosenstock takes the primordial creation-song of Amergin from early Irish myth, where poetry and the emergence into being of material form and language are joined together, and translates it to Aztec Central America and back again in daring streaks of imaginative force.[13]

The verb employed by Welch in his comment is that of translation and as Rosenstock has been active as a translator, particularly from German, it is hardly surprising that the metamorphic handling of a diverse range of cultural and literary materials should find a translational correlative. But if hybridity is to be the mark of poetry, if, in a sense, translation is an internal feature of the working out of the poetry's global concerns, where does that leave the translator of the poetry? What kind of English will he or she use? Will it specifically mark the poems as linguistically local or global?

The first point to note about Paddy Bushe, the translator of Rosenstock's second collection of selected poems, is that he is a poet who writes in Irish as well as in English.[14] Bushe then is different from other poet-translators like Paul Muldoon or Eiléan Ní Chuilleanáin whose particular status or position in translating from Irish is that their reputation rests on English-language poetry. In this respect, Paddy Bushe challenges a translation convention in being a writer from within both the Irish-language tradition and the English-language tradition who takes up a position as an English-language translator and in so doing constructs for himself a dual identity. In the first poem of the collection, 'Portráid den ealaíontóir mar yeti'/ 'A portrait of the artist as a yeti', the Irish-language references are not in any

13 Robert Welch, 'The Bengal Tiger', vii.

14 Paddy Bushe, *Poems With Amergin* (Dublin: Beaver Row Press, 1989); *Teanga* (Dublin: Coiscéim, 1990); *Counsellor* (Ballinskelligs: Sceilg Press, 1991); *Digging Towards The Light* (Dublin: Dedalus Press, 1994); *In Ainneoin na gCloch* (Dublin: Coiscéim, 2001); *Hopkins on Skellig Michael* (Dublin: Dedalus Press, 2001).

way domesticated in the English but are left as foreignizing elements in the text. So the words *sean-nós*, *Raidió na Gaeltachta* and *Údarás-funded* are not in any way anglicized nor is there any translator's footnote to elucidate the cultural referent. In the poem 'Brahms'/ 'Brahms' snatches of poetry and song are left untranslated in the English. So we have in the English poems, 'In case you'd disturb the house *Suanmhar síothach gach lá*', 'But the woman you really cared for *Measc na lilí is na mbláth*' and '*Go mbeirse, a stór, gan tuirse, gan bhrón*.' In the poem 'Loisceadh'/ 'Burning' the expression *mo léir* is left untranslated in the first line of the third stanza while the last line derives its ironic effect from the fact that the name of the protagonist of the poem, Moyshe, sounds similar when pronounced in English to the Irish-language exclamation, *Muise*. In 'Hakuin'/ 'Hakuin', the translator does not leave the Irish untranslated or use homophonic puns but he translates the Irish line by still other Irish words in the English translation. Thus, the line *Tá an áit trí chéile* is translated as 'this place is in a fierce *rírá*' and the first line of the fourth stanza *Níl dúil sa léann, sa ghaois, ná sa mhachnamh* is rendered as 'It was no *grá* for learning, or wisdom, or philosophy'. In the last long poem of the collection, 'Xolotl'/ 'Xolotl', both the Spanish italicized in the Irish and the snatch of Irish lament, which is obviously not italicized in the Irish original, make their way into the English in an undomesticated state: 'All the native women raped by the *hombres dios m'uilleagán dubh ó*'. In a poet so practised and a translator as skilful as Paddy Bushe non-translation is unlikely to be the result of incompetence or carelessness. The repetition indeed of such instances throughout the collection points to a more strategic use of the undomesticated in translation.

In the translations of Bushe the English on the whole is the standard, unmarked English of Irish Anglophones and it is not especially characterized by obvious instances of Hiberno-English. Thus, he is no Hyde signalling linguistic alterity through a recourse to a marked form of the language. On the other hand, the untranslated lines and the retention of Irish-language words such as *rírá* and *grá* and *mo léir* point to the Irish context of the texts and their difference from other texts produced in the Anglophone world. It is possible to interpret Bushe's translation strategy as at one level favouring a non-domesticating strategy in translation where the translator is anxious to foreground the linguistic and cultural otherness of the source-language text.[15] But, at another level, the move here is more radical, in that what is at work is a kind of target-culture-oriented, 'domesticating' strategy which adapts through difference rather than erasure. In other words, what Bushe is positing here is a form of Hiberno-English which is less the anglicized residue of Irish-language words and forms than a kind of hybrid plurilingualism.[16] That is to say there is no attempt to give an English orthography to the Irish words and phrases nor is there is an effort to furnish English translations of the snatches of Irish song and poetry. The distinctiveness of this form of Hiberno-English in translation is not the covert underpull of another idiom but its explicit (the words are italicized in the English) inclusion of Irish in the English target language text.

It can be argued that this shift from the strategy of Hyde to the strategy of Bushe is the result of post-independence educational policy and that Bushe's strategy reveals a degree of porosity of the English spoken in Ireland as well as linguistic hybridization in late modern Ireland. One of the avowed aims of the new State after independence was to set about the restoration of Irish as the living language of the Irish population. Much has been written about the venture and the critics are legion who point to what they perceive as the hopelessness of the enterprise.[17] However, whatever the ultimate limitations of the project, the fact is that the school-going population in the Republic has been exposed over a twelve- to thirteen-year period to Irish language, song and culture. As a result of this education, the English spoken by those who have gone through the education system is not only always already shaped by the general structures of translated Irish

15 Lawrence Venuti, *Rethinking Translation* (London: Routledge, 1992); Lawrence Venuti, *The Translator's Invisibility* (London: Routledge, 1995).

16 For a discussion of plurilingualism in heterolinguistic communication networks see Norman Denison, 'Plurilingualism and Translation' in *Theory and Practice of Translation*, ed. Lillebill Grähs, Gustav Korlén and Bertil Malmberg (Bern/Frankfurt/Las Vegas: Peter Lang, 1978), 313–19.

17 See among others Reg Hindley, *The Death of the Irish Language: a qualified obituary* (London and New York: Routledge, 1990); Tom Garvin, *Preventing the Future: why was Ireland so poor for so long* (Dublin: Gill and Macmillan, 2004); Adrian Kelly, *Compulsory Irish: Language and Education in Ireland, 1870s–1970s* (Portland, Oregon: Irish Academic Press, 2000).

in Hiberno-English but furthermore their English is porous to words and phrases from Irish which are the intelligible residue or remainders from this education. In this sense, a domestication strategy must include rather than exclude the linguistic other if it is to be truly faithful to the linguistic experiences of its potential readership. If Hyde's intention was in part to use translation to bring mainly Irish Anglophones to Irish, Bushe's translations indicate that Hyde was more successful than Kiberd suggests. The presence of unmediated hybrid plurilingualism implies a different kind of reader from the one summoned into being by the rural vernacular of Hyde's prose translations or the Kiltartanese of Lady Gregory's Molière translations.[18] That is to say, a post-independence version of Hiberno-English in the Bushe translations is predicated not on spectral traces but on overt referencing. If the poems of Rosenstock constitute a veritable global semaphore signalling other cultural experiences within the purview of Irish, the translations of the poems point to the linguistic hybridization of the Irish in late modernity in the forms of English that make it on to the page.

The perennial danger in writing about Irish affairs is the dubious virtue of Irish exceptionalism, the illusion that because something has happened in Ireland it is therefore unique to Ireland, further illustration of the doctrine of the Irish as God's Chosen People. It is important therefore to situate Irish translation developments and the emergence of specific translation strategies in the context of trends elsewhere. Frank Kermode commenting on the evolution of the Booker Prize noted that,

> The first nine Booker Prize winners included four novels by Indian novelists, or novels about India, or, failing India, other parts of the old Empire. Of the thirty or so winners of the prize to date, fewer than half are native English.[19]

18 Augusta Gregory, *The Kiltartan Molière* (Dublin: Maunsel, 1910); *Three Last Plays* (London and New York: Putnam, 1928).

19 Frank Kermode, 'In the Spirit of Mayhew', *London Review of Books* 24.8 (2002), 11–12.

In the novels of Rohinton Mistry such as *A Fine Balance* and *Family Matters*, the language of his Indian characters is given to us in English.[20] However, it is an English in which many Hindi words remain untranslated or cultural references left unexplained. Arundhati Roy's *The God of Small Things* is equally demanding of the cultural and linguistic literacy of the non-Indian reader.[21] Similarly, Mona Baker notes that in Chinua Achebe's *A Man of the People*, 'a lot of the conversations switch into Nigerian English which is so much more difficult to understand'.[22] Lawrence Venuti, for his part, has spoken of 'translingualism', in which traces of the indigenous languages are visible in the text of a dominant language through lexical and syntactical peculiarities, as well as the use of pidgins and the embedding of indigenous words and phrases.[23]

Translingualism and the embedding of indigenous words and phrases in writing from the postcolonial world is an ironic undoing of the fluency fetish in a famously translation-resistant Anglophone culture. The preoccupation with the double as other in the nineteenth century was bound up with imperialist anxieties of proximity and contamination, and the fear was always that They may be just like Us. The linguistic doubling (English plus the indigenous language) going on in these hybrid texts is at some level the return of the linguistically repressed. If English is notably failing to translate foreign texts into the language, this does not mean that translation has gone away. Rather, the difference is now internalized in the English source text as opposed to being externalized in the foreign source text. Adejunmobi has spoken of 'compositional translations'[24] where African writers are using a European language but thinking in their native language, so that a form

20 Rohinton Mistry, *A Fine Balance* (London: Faber and Faber, 1996); Rohinton Mistry, *Family Matters* (London: Faber and Faber, 2002).

21 Arundhati Roy, *The God of Small Things* (London: Flamingo, 1997).

22 Mona Baker, cited in Christine Schäffner, ed., *Translation in a Global Village* (Clevedon: Multilingual Matters, 2000), 35.

23 Lawrence Venuti, *The Scandals of Translation* (London: Routledge, 1998), 174.

24 Moradewun Adejunmobi, 'Translation and Postcolonial Identity: African Writing and European Languages', *The Translator* 4 (1998) 165.

of translation is at the heart of the creative enterprise.[25] The challenge for translators of these texts that are, in a sense, always already translated, is to retain their status as *doubly-translated* texts – once from the indigenous language to English or French or Portuguese (the original as translation) and a second time from one of these languages to another language (the translation as conventionally understood). If an effect of globalization is to make a world language like English a literary *lingua franca*, translation as an unwelcome reminder of otherness, the bothersome double, does not go away, but complicates any easy sense of unipolar linguistic or literary experiences.

Positionality in translation is not simply a question of who does the translation but where it appears and what linguistic company it keeps. Printing original source poems alongside the translations implies a different potential readership from a collection where only the translations appear. Firstly, in the imagined space of audience, the implication is that there may be a collection of readers who have a knowledge of both languages but whose mastery of one (inevitably English) is superior to the other. Secondly, and this is an alternative view, the dual-language editions recognize that competent Irish-language literacy is indeed extremely restricted and such editions preserve the integrity of the original while allowing for larger national and international readerships. This is a translational variation on the co-existence of two solitudes. Thirdly, and this is a possibility we have hinted at in the discussion of the Rosenstock translations, the translation space of the dual edition may represent a kind of laboratory for the working out of new language realities in Ireland.

Caoimhín Mac Giolla Léith in his introduction to *Ag Greadadh Bas sa Reilg* [Clapping in the Graveyard] points to the wider ambitions and more local affiliations of Louis de Paor's writing:

> De Paor's poetry is unusually expansive and welcoming. It gives due recognition to the infinite variety as well as the inalienable difference of both his physical surroundings and the people among whom he finds himself. Yet he clearly values the

25 Moradewun Adejunmobi, 'Translation and Postcolonial Identity', 163–81.

> connection with an enduring homeland and the sustaining power of those traditions and memories he associates with it.[26]

The enduring homeland is not without its tensions, however, and language can be a recurrent site of uneasy co-presence as is apparent in the poem, 'Gaeilgeoirí'/ 'Gaeilgeoirí':

> Tá gach focal mallaithe
> den teanga bhalbh seo
> ina mhianach caoch
> faoi thalamh bhodhar
> ag pléascadh gan dochar
> fénár gcosa nochtaithe.
>
> Every awful word
> of this dumb language
> is a blank land-mine
> under the careless earth,
> exploding harmlessly
> beneath our bare feet.

So how does the 'blank land-mine' of Irish affect the terrain of English in the de Paor translations and what are the translations telling us about Hiberno-English in the New Century?

The first feature to note about the translations in *Ag Greadadh Bas* is their position. They are published sequentially before the source texts. The English translations, in other words, precede the Irish originals. At one level, if we equate order with rank, then placing the English texts first implies higher status, primary position, a reversal of the standard post-Romantic privileging of the expressive originality of the source text. At another level, the decision can be justified pragmatically as determined by the primacy of the eye, which tends to fall on the right-hand rather than the left-hand page when the book is opened. The material circumstances of reading then undo the conventional link between sequence and status.

26 Caoimhín Mac Giolla Léith, 'Raiding the Vaults and Poetry's Ascendancy', in Louis de Paor, *Ag Greadadh Bas sa Reilg* (Indreabhán: Cló Iar-Chonnachta, 2005), 18.

One view of this radical re-ordering of the translation and the translated would be of course to see the collection as an abject surrender to the primacy of English in Ireland, where English translations not only become wholly palatable substitutes for Irish originals but in a sense become more important than the originals.

If we bear in mind, however, de Paor's claims about the disruptive influence of Irish, it is possible to read the practice of physical positionality differently. In other words, where land-mines are to be found is beneath the earth and what is implied by the particular sequencing of originals and translations is that rather than reading forward from the Irish original to the English translation, one is now potentially reading forward from the English translation to the Irish original. The direction forward is now into rather than out of Irish. In this way, the layered nature of Hiberno-English, those echo chambers of linguistic antecedence, are made manifest in what follows and not in what has gone before. Thus, 'wisha' in English turns out to be *Mhuise* in Irish in the poem 'Gaeilgeoirí'/ 'Gaeilgeoirí' while 'a blanket of more comforting beliefs' is revealed to be *brat seacair piseog*. In 'Believing'/ 'Creideamh', the 'sinister Masonic symbol' is a rendition of the infinitely more ambiguous *suaitheantas diamhair Máisiúnach*. In 'The Bedroom'/ 'An Seomra Codlata', the vernacular directness of 'my shitscared heroine' is a putting into English of the words, *mo bhuinneachán buí ó*, a pun on the title of the famous poem by Cathal Buí Mac Giolla Ghunna.

The mingling between the two languages is most understandably to the fore in a poem about language learning. If the initial contact of the majority of people with Irish is in a formal educational setting, then it is no accident that instruction itself becomes a meditation on the relationship between language and personal and public identity as well as being the subject of the longest footnote in the collection. 'Homework'/ 'Foghlaimeoirí' is about the more informal kind of instruction that occurs between the sheets when lovers draw on the language of the other as another resource for discovery and intimacy in much the same way Yolland and Máire Chatach do in their bilingual wooing in Brian Friel's *Translations*. Both the English translation and the Irish original contain the transliterated English versions of Irish greeting *Cén chaoi a bhfuil tú* as 'Kaykeeawillthoo' and the phrase, *Tabhair dom póg, a stór* as 'Thorampogue ashtore'. The Irish words, *clais*, *criathrach, díog, clúid, gríosach, tlú* appear unaltered and untranslated in the English (though they are translated in the footnote) and the oddness of 'belly-to-the-sun on Clochar strand' literally renders the Irish image for sunbathing, *bolg le gréin ar Thráigh an Chloichir*.

The English is always already under the influence of Irish as is only to be expected but what the 'foreign' elements demonstrate is that even the most elementary and cursory engagement with the bilingual does not leave either language unscathed. This is one of the reasons why conventional distinctions in translation theory between the 'domestic' and the 'foreign' are notions that can be misleading in their putative universal application or universalizability. That is to say, a poem and translation such as 'Homework'/ 'Foghlaimeoirí' and recurrent translation patterns in the collections of Rosenstock and de Paor show the extent to which rigid distinctions between 'domestic' and 'foreign' became problematic. Hiberno-English bears the multiple traces of a foreignized domesticity to the extent that historically for many inhabitants of the island the language of the domestic became foreign through language shift. In addition, in more recent times, the involvement of the Irish State with various aspects of bilingualism has meant that Irish Anglophones do not inhabit a wholly monoglot world. Thus, for these Anglophones what will appear as foreign to other Anglophones (Irish-language words, phrases etc.) will be part of the domestic linguistic experience.

Indeed, the very process of domestication in English for Irish poets, i.e. producing an English which is close to the lived experience of their Hiberno-English readers, can involve precisely that complication of a more universal notion of Anglophone fluency or domestication. Peter Sirr, for example, writing about a project during Cork's tenure as European Capital of Culture in 2005 where a number of European poets were translated into English by Cork-born poets notes that most of the poets relied on cribs supplied by translator intermediaries:

> Many of the translations in the series read precisely as if they were labouring under the influence of the literal versions, [they] preserve syntactic awkwardness and odd line breaks and so end up in the realm of translationese, where they could have done with

> cutting loose sufficiently to carve out a real poem in English. Some make a particular effort to domesticate the originals into a recognisable local idiom.[27]

The example that Sirr singles out as evidence of the domestication strategy are the translations by Greg Delanty of the Cypriot poet Kyriakos Charalambides and in particular the stanza from translation 'In Aramaic' which reads:

> In a short while, in less than fifty years
> they'll ask who I was, where I hailed from
> and why I hung on to a dead language. What incited
> me to take up the wonderful path
> of a lost lingo.
> Whose dantá are they in your laimheen?[28]

Even if the two Irish words are misspelt, they clearly signal a locale and a habitation for the translation in English and in this instance, it is Greek Cypriot originals rather than Irish Gaelic source poems that provide the backdrop to the translator's task.

If Hiberno-English is in one reading the child of translation, then it is only to be expected that it is in translation that we can chart the shifting territories of that particular variety of English. More broadly, the plurilingual hybridity or translingualism that is detectable in recent English-language translation practice in Ireland must relate in part to a well-documented feature of late modernity which is an overall tendency towards de-differentiation, to the dissolution of rigid separations between genders (androgynous pop stars), disciplines (the pre-eminence of biotechnology), areas of activity (virtual learning environments as a hybrid between education and computer gaming) and so on.[29] Therefore, it is hardly surprising that the variety of Hiberno-English which is emerging in the translations no longer maintains that hermetic separation on the page between the two

27 Peter Sirr, 'The Translation Muscle', *Poetry Ireland Review* 85 (2005) 71–5 (73).
28 Kyraikos Charalambides, *Selected Poems* (Cork: Southword Editions, 2005), 43.
29 David Harvey, *The Condition of Postmodernity* (Oxford: Blackwell, 1990).

language systems but that both begin to move more freely between each other in the third space of translation.

Maria Tymoczko and Colin Ireland call Ireland the 'translational island' where two cultural traditions, the English-language and the Irish-language, once separate, have now become increasingly blended and hybridized.[30] In this sense, Ireland is part of a more generalized, global condition where migratory forces are bringing any number of languages and cultures into closer contact. Robert Welch argued over a decade ago that,

> in questions of culture and tradition everything comes back to language. Whenever there is a crisis, of something vital being transacted, the words a person uses, in speech or in writing, become crucial.[31]

Something vital is being transacted in Ireland at present and translation is at the heart of the transaction though it often only appears in public accounts in a fragmented, indirect way. Evidence of the transaction is to be found in the marked shift from a country with high outward migration to a country with record levels of inward migration. In the twelve months to April 2005 Ireland had the highest levels of immigration since records on migration began in 1987. Between April 2004 and April 2005, 70,000 foreign nationals arrived in Ireland and they now make up 6% of the Irish population. It is predicted that the figure could rise to 18% of the population by 2030.[32] While public discourse on foreign nationals has largely instrumentalized their presence seeing them primarily in terms of their contribution to the economic well-being of Ireland, immigrants are of course bearers of languages and cultures. It is estimated indeed that between 160 and 210 languages are now spoken by different ethnic groups

30 Maria Tymoczko and Colin Ireland, 'Language and Tradition in Ireland: Prolegomena', in *Language and Tradition in Ireland: Continuities and Displacements*, ed. Maria Tymoczko and Colin Ireland (Amherst and Boston: University of Massachusetts Press, 2003), 1–27 (p. 20).

31 Robert Welch, *Changing States: Transformations in Modern Irish Writing* (London: Routledge, 1993), 32.

32 Kitty Holland, 'State and business faulted on immigrant response', *The Irish Times*, 13 March 2006, p. 6.

living in the Irish Republic.[33] The presence of different immigrant communities has begun to make its mark on Irish theatre as groups seek to give voice to their experience of living and working in Ireland.[34] As these groups translate themselves into the circumstances of Irish life, the nature of Hiberno-English itself is likely to change further as the domestic becomes further foreignized and the foreign domesticated.

In predicting a future for Hiberno-English it is important to bear in mind Ireland's incorporation into the turbomarket of the global English language. As the Austrian artist and critic Rainer Ganahl has pointed out, languages are 'not just products of exchange; they also encourage the exchange and commodification of most other things'.[35] Whether scientific, technical or commercial discourse is produced in English, German, French or Yoruba 'has an impact on university studies, research, corporate investments, and decision and definition making of all kinds'.[36] A recent report, which indicated that US investment in Ireland in 2003 was two times greater than total US investment in China, pointed out that a 'large, English-speaking labour force' was a decisive factor influencing the investment decisions of US technology firms.[37] It is astonishing therefore, in all the debate around Ireland and the Boston/Berlin axis, that so little attention is devoted to the linguistic dimension to Ireland's relationships with the rest of the world. The 'work being done in other languages' is now happening not only beyond the nation's borders but within them and translation is likely to be the first port of call in the new odyssey of Hiberno-English.

33 Michael Cronin, 'Babel Atha Cliath: The Languages of Dublin', *New Hibernia Review* 8.4 (Winter 2004) 9–22.

34 See the excellent article by Jason King, 'Interculturalism and the Irish Theatre: the Portrayal of Immigrants on the Irish Stage', *The Irish Review* 33 (Spring 2005) 23–39.

35 Rainer Ganahl, 'Free Markets: Language, Commodification and Art', in Emily Apter ed., *Translation in a Global Market*, special issue of *Public Culture* 13.1 (Winter 2001) 23–38 (27).

36 Ganahl, 'Free Markets', 28.

37 Conor O'Clery, 'US invested twice as much in Ireland as in China', *The Irish Times*, 18 May 2004.

MICHELLE WOODS

Love and Other Subtitles: Comedic and Abusive Subtitling in *Annie Hall* and *Wayne's World*

> In Europe, his films are greeted and loved there as equals, all of the same stature. In America, some are hits, some are flops. Critics draw sharp distinctions among them. 'Maybe they gain something in translation', he says wryly.
> — WOODY ALLEN[1]

Alvy Singer and Wayne Campbell are smitten, and they try to convey their love to Annie Hall and Cassandra Wong. As both are awkward communicators they cannot speak of love; instead Alvy talks about Annie's photographs and the 'aesthetic criteria' of the 'new art form'; Wayne talks about his ex-girlfriend Stacey and her 'self-nullifying behavior'. The women respond and all four, in these mostly monolingual films, speak in subtitles. In *Annie Hall* (1977), those subtitles reveal what the characters are really thinking ('I wonder what she looks like naked'), and in *Wayne's World* (1992), they translate the fluent Cantonese that the slacker Wayne can suddenly speak. Can we read this comedic use of subtitling in ostensibly monolingual English-language films as a form of what Abé Mark Nornes has described as 'abusive subtitling'?[2] If so, does it suggest models of subtitling for translating films?

1 'My Bust Up with Mia Would Have Made a Great Movie'. Interview with Woody Allen, *The Guardian*, 24 November 2000. http://www.guardian.co.uk/film/2000/nov/24/culture.features. Accessed 3 June 2010.

2 Abé Mark Nornes, 'For an Abusive Subtitling', *Film Quarterly* 52.3 (Spring 1999), 17–34.

Annie Hall, written and directed by Woody Allen, won four Oscars after its release in 1977, including best movie, best director and best female lead (for Diane Keaton playing the eponymous Annie Hall). Described as a 'nervous romance', the film follows the birth and death of the love affair between the comedian Alvy Singer and the newcomer to town, Annie Hall.[3] But in narrative style it is a 'dismantling of romantic comedy' that 'create[s] an unsettling vision of the emotional battlefield of modern romance. The film offers many of the scenes conventionally found in a romantic comedy, but disassembles the structures that traditionally organize their meaning'.[4] In other words, the non-linear structure of the film and use of a mixture of filmic techniques foreground the artificiality of the medium and, Frank Krutnik argues, the disintegration of previously-held norms of the narrative line of the romance genre and of the language of romance itself. Allen's use of subtitles in one of the first love scenes is part of this postmodern critique of the modern romance.

Similarly, the more lowbrow *Wayne's World* (1992), written by Mike Myers and directed by Penelope Spheeris, uses postmodern filmic techniques that consistently break down the fourth wall of film realism, presenting fantasy sequences, mock endorsements, straight-to-camera asides, unexpected subtitles, and three alternative endings. Born from two characters, Wayne and Garth, who first appeared on the US TV comedy sketch series, *Saturday Night Live*, the film follows the story of their cable-TV show shot in Wayne's parents' basement, their show being picked up by a ruthless TV executive, and Wayne falling in love with the 'megababe' local rock-star Cassandra Wong. The heavily referential, 'self-reflexive and parodic' film was a box-office hit.[5] It spawned a sequel *Wayne's World 2*

3 Peter William Evans and Celestino Deleyto, 'Introduction: Surviving Love', in *Terms of Endearment: Hollywood Romantic Comedy of the 1980s and 1990s* (Edinburgh: Edinburgh University Press, 1998), 1–19 (p. 1).

4 Frank Krutnik, 'Love Lies: Romantic Fabrication in Contemporary Romantic Comedy', in *Terms of Endearment: Hollywood Romantic Comedy of the 1980s and 1990s*, 15–26 (p. 20).

5 Jeanne Dubino, 'Wayne's World: Postmodern or Nostalgic?', *Popular Culture Review*, 6.2 (1995), 145–53 (145).

the following year, as well as a number of catchphrases that went, to use an anachronistic phrase, viral: 'Excellent', 'Schwing', 'NOT!' (the latter to convey ironic detachment from any previous statement).[6]

That these terms entered the lexicon shows the plasticity of English and is suggestive of how we might read monolingual US cinema as being linguistically heterogeneous, especially given the characters' different ethnic and social backgrounds: Annie Hall the Wisconsin WASP falls for Alvy Singer, a Coney Island Jew; the blue-collar white Wayne Campbell falls for the Chinese-American Cassandra Wong (played by the Filipina-American actress Tia Carrera). If there is a sense in both films that each sex speaks its own 'genderlect', that there is a fundamental need for translation between the sexes, there is also a sense that people from different socio-ethnic American backgrounds also might need to translate the meaning of another's words.[7] In other words, 'translation is as much an intralingual as an interlingual phenomenon' and even films in cultures perceived to be monolingual might reveal 'how linguistically diverse and culturally variegated societies are'.[8] That both films use subtitling foregrounds this notion and makes the audience aware of the resistance to comprehension even in the act of declaring love.

Both films also make the audience aware of subtitling as an act that has been given a cultural meaning in itself. The films, in their comedic utilization of them, suggest that subtitles signal foreignness and intellectual heft (in negative terms they are also 'purist and elitist').[9] In *Annie Hall*, this expectation is usurped by the basic nature of the characters' thought (in correlation to the intellectual conversation they are having) while in *Wayne's World* the subtitles indicate an intellectual eloquence, reinforced by Wayne suddenly speaking another language fluently, that Wayne cannot

6 See Jesse T. Sheidlower and Jonathan E. Lighter, 'A Recent Coinage (Not!)', *American Speech*, 68.2 (Summer, 1993), 213–18.

7 Deborah Tannen, *You Just Don't Understand: Women and Men in Conversation* (New York: Harper, 2007), 42.

8 Michael Cronin, *Translation Goes to the Movies* (London and New York: Routledge, 2009), 57, 62.

9 Nornes, 'For an Abusive Subtitling', 19.

match in his native tongue. The foreign language and subtitles make Wayne more intelligent and therefore more alluring, a kind of Cyrano effect.

In deconstructing our expectations of what subtitles portend, the films also say something about the stagnancy, or at least conservatism, of the form and audience expectations of subtitles. They are there for functionality and, given the speed of film, require brevity and succinctness.[10] They are there to be seen and not heard, not expected to bring notice to themselves and only do so when the audience sees glaring mistakes.[11] Given the difficulty of translating 'culture bound' texts[12] and the technical requirements for brevity, the practice, Nornes argues 'smoothes over its textual violence and domesticates all otherness while it pretends to bring the audience to an experience of the foreign', and so 'all subtitles are corrupt'.[13] Nornes bases his notion of 'abusive subtitling' on Philip E. Lewis's call for 'abusive fidelity' in translation. Lewis acknowledges that texts contain elements of untranslatability and rather than smoothing over these 'nubs' of resistance he argues that the translator should engage and highlight them.[14] This notion was also popularized by Lawrence Venuti in his call for 'foreignizing' strategies of translation.[15] 'Put more concretely', Nornes writes,

> the abusive subtitler uses textual and graphic abuse – that is, experimentation with language and its grammatical, morphological, and visual qualities – to bring the fact of translation from its position of obscurity, to critique the imperial politics that ground corrupt practices while ultimately leading the viewer to the foreign original being reproduced in the darkness of the theater. This original is not an origin threat-

10 Birgit Nedergaard-Larsen, 'Culture-Bound Problems in Subtitling', *Perspectives, Studies in Translatology*, 2 (1993), 207–42 (213).

11 Nornes, 'For an Abusive Subtitling', 17.

12 Nedergaard-Larsen, 'Culture-Bound Problems in Subtitling', 207–42.

13 Nornes, 'For an Abusive Subtitling', 17–18.

14 Philip E. Lewis, 'The Measure of Translation Effects' in *Difference in Translation*, ed. by Joseph F. Graham (Ithaca and London: Cornell University Press, 1985), 31–62 (p. 43).

15 Lawrence Venuti, *The Translator's Invisibility: A History of Translation* (London and New York: Routledge, 2008), 18.

> ened by contamination, but a locus of the individual and the international which can potentially turn the film into an *experience of translation*.[16]

Nornes gives some examples of abusive subtitling: he writes of how the English subtitler of Jean Eustache's French New Wave film, *La Maman et la putain* (1973) interrupted the 'transparency of the subtitles' with 'the bracketed note *[Untranslatable French Pun]*' or how Rob Young translated obscene expressions in Yamamoto Masashi's film *Tenamonya konekushon* as '!%&$#!@!!' which underlines 'the linguistic playfulness of the original scenario' and also, unlike many other subtitlers, does not simply ignore or censor foul language. Finally, he cites the example of '*anime* fandom' where fans provide amateur translations for *anime* on the web and provide 'abusive subtitles *quite by instinct*' using different sized fonts and colours to denote different moods and dialects, subtitles covering the screen, the retention of untranslatable Japanese words in English subtitles and footnotes.[17]

So, as Nornes argues, there are possibilities for more experimental subtitling strategies, but, of course, the difficulty lies in persuading mainstream commercial cinema to adopt any of them, when it fears the ability to sell foreign films to English-language audiences, though increasing consumption on the internet may change this (*anime* fandom being an example). Nornes suggests, however, that experimentation with abusive subtitling may begin with genres such as animation, art films, documentaries and comedies, 'texts that are themselves transgressive'.[18]

Nornes points to potential in abusive subtitling in addressing comedy (the untranslatable French pun, the symbols instead of swearing) but does so in interlingual terms; others have pointed to the difficulty in translating comedy in film because of space, cultural differences or censorship.[19] But what happens when subtitling *is* the joke? When our anxieties about

16 Nornes, 'For an Abusive Subtitling', 18.

17 Nornes, 'For an Abusive Subtitling', 28, 30, 32.

18 Nornes, 'For an Abusive Subtitling', 32.

19 See Katja Pelsmaekers and Fred Van Besien, 'Subtitling Irony: *Blackadder* in Dutch', *The Translator* 8.2 (2002), 241–66. See in the same issue, Jeroen Vandaele, '"Funny Fictions": Francoist Translation Censorship of Two Billy Wilder Films', 267–302.

gender, social and ethnic difference, misunderstanding, class and intellect are played out on screen through subtitles as the joke? And when this use of subtitles highlights the foreign in the domestic mainstream movie? From the fact that both *Annie Hall* and *Wayne's World* were successful films and played with subtitles, can we infer that an English-speaking audience might be more ready to accept experimentation with subtitles, and the concomitant presence of difference in domestic language and identity, than commercial cinema thinks?

The medium is the message

After an embarrassed silence, Alvy Singer says to Annie, 'So, did you shoot those photographs in there or what?'. They are standing on the terrace of her Manhattan apartment. More or less strangers, they are gauging their attraction to each other and Alvy wants to impress; he inhabits the register of New York intellectual, even though we find out in the film that he is an outsider from that milieu, having been born into a more working-class Jewish family who live under the Coney Island Cyclone (a rollercoaster in the sea-side theme park). Annie, a newcomer to the city (from Wisconsin) feels obliged to sustain the intellectual register and the conversation goes like this:

> ANNIE: Yeah, yeah, I sorta dabble around, you know.
>
> ALVY: They're ... they're ... they're wonderful, you know. They have ... they have, uh ... a ... a quality.
>
> ANNIE: Well, I–I–I would–I would like to take a serious photography course soon.
>
> ALVY: Photography's interesting, 'cause, you know, it's–it's a new art form, and a, uh, a set of aesthetic criteria have not emerged yet.
>
> ANNIE: Aesthetic criteria? You mean, whether it's, uh, good photo or not?
>
> ALVY: The–the medium enters in as a condition of the art form itself. That's–
>
> ANNIE: Well, well, I ... to me–I ... I mean, it's–it's–it's all instinctive, you know. I mean, I just try to uh, feel it, you know? I try to get a sense of it and not think about it so much.

ALVY: Still, still we– You need a set of aesthetic guide lines to put it in social perspective, I think.
ANNIE: Well, I don't know. I mean, I guess – I guess you must be sorta late, huh?

The conversation is understandable to the English-language audience both in its surface meaning (the discussion of Annie's photography) and in its tone and subtexts (the awkward flirtation in the hesitancies; Alvy's attempt to impress Annie with his apparent expertise; Annie's discomfort with the intellectual register). Why then, does Allen add subtitles? Krutnik argues that the 'subtitles playfully expose the gap between what they want to say and the disengaging platitudes they actually mouth. Alvy and Annie are highly self-conscious players of a scenario of romantic initiation'.[20] The subtitles, in other words, serve to emphasize the emptiness of the language both use; the tone and register of the language is more meaningful. The subtitles let us read what the characters are actually thinking:

ANNIE: Yeah, yeah, I sorta dabble around, you know.
[I dabble? Listen to me–what a jerk!]
ALVY: They're ... they're ... they're wonderful, you know. They have ... they have, uh ... a ... a quality.
[You are a great-looking girl.]
ANNIE: Well, I–I–I would–I would like to take a serious photography course soon.
[He probably thinks I'm a yo-yo.]
ALVY: Photography's interesting, 'cause, you know, it's–it's a new art form, and a, uh, a set of aesthetic criteria have not emerged yet.
[I wonder what she looks like naked?]
ANNIE: Aesthetic criteria? You mean, whether it's, uh, good photo or not?
[I'm not smart enough for him. Hang in there.]
ALVY: The–the medium enters in as a condition of the art form itself. That's–
[I don't know what I'm saying–she senses I'm shallow.]
ANNIE: Well, well, I ... to me–I ... I mean, it's–it's–it's all instinctive, you know. I mean, I just try to uh, feel it, you know? I try to get a sense of it and not think about it so much.
[God, I hope he doesn't turn out to be a shmuck like the others.]

20 Krutnik, 'Love Lies: Romantic Fabrication in Contemporary Romantic Comedy', 21.

ALVY: Still, still we– You need a set of aesthetic guide lines to put it in social perspective, I think.
[Christ, I sound like FM radio. Relax.]
ANNIE: Well, I don't know. I mean, I guess–I guess you must be sorta late, huh?

Part of the immediate humour in seeing the subtitled thoughts alongside their conversation is in the contrapuntal registers; we might have sensed without the subtitles that they are both inhabiting the foreign (to their backgrounds) intellectual register but now we see that their real selves are thinking in an idiomatic and more immediate way. The brevity and forthrightness of their thoughts contrast with the verbosity and longer length of the more intellectual conversation. This speaks to the medium itself, the subtitles that demand, as we have seen, brevity and in this sense, Allen is parodying the limits of this brevity, and reflecting what he is doing in the conversation itself. If in photography, 'the medium enters in as a condition of the art form itself', so it does with subtitles. He is using the limits of the form to extrapolate on its meaning.

He also parodies the ideas of a foreign movie in which we might expect profound and elitist statements just because it is in a foreign language and the notion that subtitles are only presenting us with what amounts to the gist of the original. Alvy is and is not part of the New York intellectual world; he attempts to broaden Annie's horizons by introducing her to intellectual texts: books (all with death in the title) and his favourite foreign film, Marcel Ophül's 1969 documentary about collaboration and resistance in Vichy France, *The Sorrow and the Pity*, but in the queue for the film we see his increasing irritation towards a Columbia professor pontificating behind them about Fellini, Beckett and Marshall McLuhan; after telling Annie that he's just a 'comparatively normal ... guy raised in Brooklyn' Alvy turns on the academic and tells him he knows nothing about McLuhan. The professor tells him he teaches a course on McLuhan and, so, Alvy pulls McLuhan out from the wings of the frame, asking him what he thinks of the professor's assertions: McLuhan tells the professor that he 'knows nothing of my work' and Alvy turns to camera and says 'If only life were really like that'. McLuhan is most famous for his proposition that 'the medium is the message', and here Allen is playing with the limits of fictionality and representation, revealing film in its state as a medium.[21] Similarly, in foregrounding the subtitles between Alvy and Annie, he plays with the audience expectations of the medium of subtitles: before we see them, we expect already what they mean (intellectual, profound and foreign conversation).

The subtitles begin after an embarrassed silence: Annie has just said, forthrightly, 'You're what Grammy Hall would call a real Jew' and adds that her 'Grammy' 'hates Jews'. After being reminded of his outsider status, Alvy changes the subject and talks about her photography in the intellectual register he attempts. The subtitles signify his entrance into another foreign world, into the seduction of Annie, who 'represents both forbidden fruit and the incarnation of the American dream'.[22] Alvy has already picked up on her cultural otherness, to him, through linguistic markers. Before they go on to the terrace Alvy finds Sylvia Plath's *Ariel* on Annie's bookcase. She describes the poetry as 'neat'; 'Neat?', Alvy says, 'Uh, I hate to tell yuh, this is nineteen seventy-five, you know that "neat" went out, I would say, at the turn of the century'. 'Neat' does not simply signify the past, but a past of homogenous WASP-ishness; Alvy is at once attracted to the charm of it and the knowledge of it as a linguistic marker of a bygone era. Alvy is living in a more heterogeneous Americanness of 'nineteen seventy-five' where there might be a combative relationship between classes, identities and gender but there is also a sense of dynamism and evolution that is shown linguistically.

In the official language they speak out loud, in the subtitled scene, both Alvy and Annie inhabit an intellectual register, and Annie is vaguer, more stereotypically WASP female, feeling art instead of thinking it through. Yet in the subtitles, she comes across as more forceful, first against herself: 'Listen to me – what a jerk!', 'I'm a yo-yo'; and then against Alvy and men in general: 'hope he doesn't turn out to be schmuck like the others'. Her

21 Marshall McLuhan, *Understanding Media: The Extensions of Man* (Cambridge Mass.: MIT Press, 1994), 7.

22 Foster Hirsch, *Love, Sex, Death and the Meaning of Life: The Films of Woody Allen* (New York: McGraw Hill, 1981), 112.

use of the Yiddish term *schmuck* is funny, because it is unexpected from the WASP Wisconsiner, but it shows also that Annie is becoming a New Yorker, in adopting the term heard locally. It also suggests that the English language is in flux: if *neat* is nostalgic, *schmuck* is the language of 'nineteen seventy-five'. But similarly, the Jewish Alvy, in his next subtitled thought: 'Christ, I sound like FM radio', invokes specifically Christian blasphemy that has become generic in contemporary language and, in effect, evolves another meaning for what it represents, an outburst of frustration. The language of the subtitles is not only more demotic than the language the characters speak publicly, it also opens up the possibilities of deconstructing the identity stereotypes of the two lovers. It does not result in a linguistic melting-pot but identifies resistant cultural terms that are swapped and embedded with new and different meanings.

For Foster Hirsch, the 'conflict between Jew and gentile' in Allen's films is a dramatization of 'the ongoing battle between the sexes'.[23] In a sense, he is right. There is a connection between the sense of difference in their gender and ethnic identities but it is not a conflict or battle between these separate identities but rather, I would argue, a negotiation. Alvy's discourse on the aesthetics of photography and his concomitant subtitled thoughts seem, at first, to be stereotypical of the dominant male ('I wonder what she looks like naked?') but it plays with that stereotype, first, because it expects men to be thinking about sex even at their most eloquent, but also because these are the thoughts of a pint-sized, glasses-wearing weakling in front of a beautiful, independent woman. Alvy has, in fact, just joked about his relation to male gender telling Annie that he did not have a shower after their tennis game because, 'I don't like to show my body to a man of my gender'. In doing so, he seems to follow the feminized stigmitization of Jewish males.[24] Annie, too, shows some gender mixing in her language; a steelier side in the subtitles using terms like *jerk* and *schmuck*, and in their formal conversation adopting a stereotypically female role, a little

23 Hirsch, *Love, Sex, Death and the Meaning of Life*, 141.

24 Sander L. Gilman, *Franz Kafka, the Jewish Patient* (New York and London: Routledge, 1995), 39.

submissive and hesitant. She is also wearing male clothes: a tie, waistcoat and trousers and in doing so, subverting both the WASP female identity and images of manhood. Whereas they seem to follow male and female roles in the dialogue, in the subtitles they exchange those roles: Annie starts out angry at herself, moves through insecurity, then anger at Alvy and men in general, thus moving from a stereotyped female insecurity to a stereotyped male anger. Alvy begins thinking about sex, but then starts to become insecure: 'she senses I'm shallow', 'I sound like FM radio'. It is not that they swap gender or ethnic identities but that there seems to be a negotiation between these identities, thrown into play as the prescriptions of romance transform them, a change that is markered by the subtitles.

Subtitles fundamentally function to allow us to understand a foreign text and the strategy has been, according to Nornes, to falsely universalize the message through domestication, so that the foreign is just like us. On the other hand, 'rather than smoothing the rough edges of foreignness', he argues,

> rather than converting everything into easily consumable meaning, the abusive subtitles always direct spectators back to the original text. Abusive subtitles circulate between the foreign and the familiar, the known and the unknown ...[25]

The use of subtitles in this scene in *Annie Hall* confounds our expectations, primarily for comedic effect, making us secret *entendeurs*. But Allen is also bringing audience attention to the use of subtitles, to the medium as message, and subverting those expectations (of seriousness, of abstract profundity, of instrumentalism). In addition, he is also using the subtitles to make the viewer or *entendeur* aware of the foreign in the familiar. While on the face of it we are watching a seduction scene and have our preconceived stereotypes of gender roles and Americanness, or New Yorkness, and of class, the subversive subtitles play with, and challenge, these preconceptions. So while we identify with the universalism of the situation (flirtation, attraction, love) and perhaps for moments see Alvy as the 'neurotic Everyman',[26]

25 Nornes, 'For an Abusive Subtitling', 32.
26 Hirsch, *Love, Sex, Death and the Meaning of Life*, 17.

He is '*just like us*' and this, Hirsch argues, is the 'lesson, the appeal' of Allen's comedy while the subtitles also destabilize that assurance.[27] Love may seem to represent an ultimate understanding between selves and identities, but the subtitles indicate that it is also the locus of misunderstanding between individuals, and even that misunderstanding is the primary language of love. The subtitles are not a direct or faithful translation of the characters' words because listening is an ever-changing interpretation due to the flux of emotion and the sly morphing of identity.

Wayne's words

'To label me is to negate me', Wayne Campbell says, in Cantonese, to Cassandra Wong. He is referring to their psychological analysis of his ex-girlfriend Stacy who is kissing a man behind them in order to make Wayne jealous. Wayne's sudden transformation, from slacker dude with an infantile attitude to women to a sensitive intellectual speaking in a foreign language with delicacy to a woman, is unexpected and funny. Wayne has fallen in love with Cassandra after watching her sing with her band at the Gasworks rock club; he uses the same words about her straight to camera that he does about the white Fender guitar he admires in a shop window: 'Oh yes, she will be mine'. Delivered in a mock-portentous voice, the comparison invites the viewer to see Wayne objectifying Cassandra as an 'exotic rock and roll "babe"'.[28] Cassandra, when he first sees her, is dressed as an eroticized object: dressed all in white (like the guitar), she has a plunging neckline and short shorts, holding up suspenders and stockings. She seems to step out of this stereotype as she comes off stage and breaks up a fight with some karate moves. 'I love this woman', Wayne says

27 Hirsch, *Love, Sex, Death and the Meaning of Life*, 15.

28 Mark S. Graybill, '"Nothing Really Matters": Inauthenticity, Intertextuality, and Rock in Wayne's World', *CEA Critic*, 66.2–3 (2004), 39–46 (40).

to camera, but then attempts a pick-up line when she comes to the bar: 'Rough night, huh? Everybody's kung fu fighting'. He winces just after saying this, realizing not only the lameness of the joke, but also that the reference to Carl Douglas's 1974 one-hit wonder, 'Kung-Fu Fighting', might be taken as reductively racist since Cassandra is a Hong Kong immigrant. Unimpressed, and seemingly used to the sexual and racial innuendos, she says: 'Yeah. Well, nice meeting you'.

In order to get it right the next time he meets her, Wayne starts listening to Cantonese on his Walkman, initially scaring his side-kick Garth with his attempts at Cantonese. 'Stop it! You're scaring me!', Garth says, until he realizes what these noises are: 'Oh cool. You're learning Cassandra's language'. Garth's fear of the sound of the unintelligible foreign language is assuaged when he realizes its purpose – that this unnamed language 'Cassandra's language' is the language of love. Wayne is literally trying to speak *her* language. In a film full of fantasy scenes, spoofed, this is another fantasy and it takes one shot of Wayne listening to language tapes on his Walkman to make him fluent.

The next time he meets Cassandra he asks if they can 'talk' and they go up on the roof of a warehouse where her gig has just taken place, a nod to the cheesy romance convention of the rooftop seduction. Wayne compliments her band in slang 'you guys wail', and tells her they'll 'make it'. Cassandra responds in slightly bizarre, idiomatic slang: 'And if a frog had wings, he wouldn't bump his ass hopping', but it reflects the bizzareness of the hermetic slang world created by Wayne, Garth and their followers (slang that gains linguistic currency beyond the film after its box-office success). Wayne asks her where she learnt her English: 'College', she says, 'and the Police Academy movies'. The postmodern mixture of high and low (the accepted place to learn a language and the utterly populist, sexist and crass world of low moviedom) is funny but also contains a grain of truth, namely that language is learnt in the world around us as well as formally and that films have a role in language-learning. 'I have something to say', Wayne says, as the romantic music reaches a crescendo and he tells her she is pretty in Cantonese. She tells him he is handsome and that she's amazed he can speak the language with such a good accent. That they have begun to speak with subtitles is convenient, as Wayne's stalker girlfriend, Stacy, has followed them up to the rooftop and is making out with a random rocker to try and make Wayne jealous. 'Who is she?', Cassandra asks, and the Cantonese and subtitles allow them to gossip about Stacy, letting us become privy to that gossip, except suddenly their subtitled conversation has entered the kind of clichéd pseudo-intellectual register of the self-help manual:

> CASS: She has very nice legs but no self-esteem.
> WAYNE: The irony is, I feel partly responsible for her self-nullifying behavior.
> CASS: You're allowing yourself to be victimized. Perhaps you haven't been effectively assertive.
> WAYNE: I've made a confident declaration in defense of my rights.

As with *Annie Hall*, the subtitles seem to herald an elision of normative gender roles: Cassandra is the one who notices the 'nice legs' and tells Wayne he's being 'victimized' and is not 'effectively assertive'. Wayne is all sensitivity and thus thrust into the expectations of the female role: 'I feel partly responsible for her self-nullifying behavior'. They, Wayne and Cassandra, become aware of the subtitles as Wayne's brief comment in Cantonese becomes stretched over a number of subtitles and both remain silent:

> WAYNE: but, it doesn't seem to do any good. [Wayne looks at camera, silent, waiting]. If I help her out of feelings of obligation, I may find myself resenting her [Wayne looks at watch, looks back at camera, still not speaking] Besides she's a psycho hose beast.

Both self-consciously wait for the subtitled version of Wayne's brief statement to end, and the joke is on the mechanism of subtitles. Usually so brief and even reductively to-the-point, here the subtitles take over and become a verbose articulation of Wayne's statement that takes so long that Wayne impatiently looks at his watch. He makes the audience aware of the mechanism of the subtitles, our dependence on them for understanding, and also subverts our expectations of the timely, brief subtitle. In terms of the content of the subtitles, gender roles seem reversed since in Wayne's words there is a mixture of the expected female normative role of slightly injured romantic sensitivity: 'it doesn't seem to do any good', 'feelings of obligation', 'I may find myself', curtailed by the adolescent assertive slang at the end: 'she's a psycho hose beast'.

Nicole Matthews argues that the main purpose of the scene is 'to spoof the use of subtitles in foreign-language films' and in doing so, the film 'undermine[s] plausible characterisation' and 'breaks the classical-realist illusion of an invisible fourth wall by showing that these characters are aware they are in a film'.[29] The scene posits the low culture movie that it is against a pastiche of what we expect from 'art movies', that is to say, profound dialogue markered by subtitles.[30] In fact, the film, as Mark Graybill argues, 'exude[s] silliness, but not mindlessness'.[31] It is not simply a 'spoof of the use of subtitles' but makes us, the audience, aware that we collude in expectations not only of what subtitles represent but also what they say. Cassandra and Wayne get to the heart of this as the scene concludes:

> CASS: That is very funny. But labeling people can be very dangerous.
> WAYNE: Was it Kierkegaard or Dick Van Patten who said 'If you label me, you negate me'?

Cassandra, the exoticized 'megababe', deconstructs the stereotyping of her character here.[32] She is labelled, we have labelled her, and we are invited to laugh at the process of that labelling (through the juxtaposition of her clothes with her tough action, through her tough and assertive words here in comparison with stereotyped notions of Asian womanhood, through Wayne's lack of racial sensitivity, and so on). Wayne's inability to discern between the philosopher Kierkegaard and the sit-com actor Dick Van Patten points to the level of our current cultural analysis that is reduced to de-contextualized aphorism that at once makes us comfortable in its apparent wisdom (since we are familiar with it) but also makes us uncomfortable because of its sly elision of intellectual context (it remains foreign).

29 Nicole Matthews, *Comic Politics: Gender in Hollywood Comedy After the New Right* (Manchester and New York: Manchester University Press, 2000), 19–20.

30 Matthews, *Comic Politics*, 20.

31 Graybill, '"Nothing Really Matters"', 39.

32 Dubino, 'Wayne's World: Postmodern or Nostalgic?', 149.

The humanist assertion is nice, but somehow nostalgic. The characters' subtitled call for not stereotyping or labelling people challenges us as we are in the act of doing just that: surprised at Wayne and Cassandra's sudden intellectuality, fluency and embrace of the foreign.

Wayne's impatient look at his watch as the subtitles keep going on also makes the viewer aware that someone else is subtitling their conversation. The transparency is lost as we are made aware of the effort of translation, how to transfer a 'pithy Cantonese phrase' into meaningful English.[33] We are left with the sense that the subtitler has added in material, with Wayne's final distinctive phrasing, 'psycho hose beast' (which he used earlier in the film about Stacy). The invisible translator makes himself or herself suddenly visible because of too many subtitles, for a moment taking over the visual stage with a verbal weapon. Nornes notes how mistakes are what we remember about subtitles, but here, there is an embrace of mistake, it becomes an instrument of power.[34]

Mike Myers has, in fact, returned to subtitling as a visual and aural gag in two more films: the sequel to *Wayne's World*, *Wayne's World 2* (1993) and the third film of his Austin Powers series, *Austin Powers: Goldmember* (2002). In *Wayne's World 2*, the subtitles again center around Wayne's wooing of Cassandra. This time, the subtitles are needed because her father, Jeff Wong (James Hong), has arrived from Hong Kong to meet Wayne. After an awkward introduction, Wayne says, 'Allow me to speak your native tongue, Mr. Wong' and the men begin a negotiation about Cassandra's future in Cantonese with subtitles. Cassandra is dressed in a traditional Chinese silk dress and when she raises an objection to the negotiation, her father says: 'Quiet. Adult speaking'. Wayne challenges her father's patriarchal attitude in Cantonese: 'With all respect, Jeff. In our culture, women are allowed to make their own decisions', even though he has shown his own tendencies in opening the scene by ogling Cassandra in her traditional dress and saying, 'You look hot'. Cassandra's father challenges Wayne to a fight, and Wayne answers: 'If we are to fight I think it would be better if

33 Matthews, *Comic Politics*, 20.

34 Nornes, 'For an Abusive Subtitling', 17.

we were dubbed and not in subtitles'. What begins is a pastiche of old kung fu films, with Wayne and Jeff Wong flying through the air and twirling swords in order to fight for the now mostly passive Cassandra, but Myers also plays with how those kung fu films entered American culture: through hasty dubbing that underscored the needs of the target culture. So, Jeff Wong is dubbed into a deep, masculine American voice, as is Wayne and the fight is thus made ridiculously male, the voices at odds with the visual images of the men. To underscore this, the dubbing is unsynchronized, so that at times the dubbed voices speak when the characters do not, and, in general, the dubbed voices do not match the movements of the characters' mouths. Myers nods to the cultural appropriation of kung fu films, consumed in America via dubious ventriloquism that perhaps consolidated the construction of Hollywood maleness and of the Hollywood other – the controlled vision of male Asianness through populist fight scenes. Wayne wins Jeff Wong's approval through the fight ('Zang!' he says finishing the scene, and going back to subtitles). In this way he at once affirms male stereotypes of fighting for the woman – being dubbed in the fight scene because they don't really need words – and at the same time subverting the stereotypes by pointing visually to the absurdity of the visual fight and to the manipulation, through dubbing and domestic acculturation (the deep, masculine voices) of the aural construction of these males.

In Myers' James Bond spoof, *Austin Powers: Goldmember* (2002), the characters physically interact with the subtitles in one scene in which Austin Powers, an improbable English secret agent with bad teeth brought back from the swinging sixties and his sidekick, Foxxy Cleopatra (Beyoncé Knowles), are trying to get information about Austin's kidnapped father from a Japanese industrialist Mr. Roboto (Nobu Matsuhisa). Foxxy, it turns out, speaks fluent Japanese and so the subtitles appear. But the problem is that they are in white and, so, the ends of the sentences in the subtitles keep disappearing into the background making the sentences appear rude to Austin Powers who reads the subtitles while Mr. Roboto speaks. Mr Roboto begins by offering Austin some food from a bowl on his desk: 'Please eat some shit', the subtitles read. 'Please eat what?', Austin exclaims. 'Wait', Foxxy says, and moving one of the bowls away from the subtitles, she leans over the subtitles pointing to them with her hand. 'It says: "Please eat some shitake mushrooms"' and we as viewers see the whole title, previously obscured by the bowl. Mr. Roboto then moves over to some shelves with black and white files, and his answer to Austin's query about his father is obscured because we can only see the part of the subtitle with the black files behind it: 'Your ass is happy', it reads. 'No', Foxxy says, as she pulls a black filing cabinet down, so we can see the whole subtitle: 'Your assignment is an unhappy one', it reads. Mr. Roboto then moves over to a geisha wearing white and the subtitle reads: 'I have a huge rod'. The geisha seems shocked and Austin exclaims, 'Nice potty mouth, dirtbag', but the geisha has moved and we see the whole subtitle, 'I have a huge rodent problem'. ('A little off topic', he adds, 'but important nonetheless'). 'Why don't I just speak English?', Mr. Roboto finally says, and Austin throws up his hands: 'That would be a good idea, now wouldn't it?', he says, 'That way I wouldn't misread the subtitles making it seem that you're saying things that are dirty'.

Of course, the Austin Powers franchise is all about potty humour (Mike Myers' homage to his English father who introduced him to British comedy), but it points to two elements: first, the technical and spatial difficulties of subtitling and secondly, the disparity between message and interpretation. Austin Powers sees what he expects to see; he is coming to the subtitles with a preconceived interpretation. The breaking down of the fourth wall of realism, wherein the characters themselves see, read and interact with the subtitles is doubly ironic because they – or at least Austin Powers – are reading only what they see. His inability to see the full white subtitles on black backgrounds may, in addition, be related to race in a film – and film franchise – that plays with racial stereotypes and the act of that stereotyping, perhaps summed up by Austin's kidnapped father, Nigel Powers (Michael Caine), in his comment: 'There are two things I can't stand in this world. People who are intolerant of other people's cultures ... and the Dutch', funny in itself because the evil character is Dutch, subverting the racial typology, and our expectations, of Hollywood action moves, whose evil characters are invariably Russian or Arab. Foxxy is a pastiche of a blaxploitation diva as well as a Bond Girl in her scanty clothing, but she is the one who interprets the subtitles by pulling down black backgrounds, so that some form of understanding can happen between Austin Powers and Mr. Roboto.

Goldmember made $300 million worldwide; like *Wayne's World* it became a huge comedic success.[35] That these films used subtitles, successfully, and, I would argue, abusively, may speak to our own fears as an audience of subtitles. The films, like *Annie Hall*, make making fun of and subvert the perceived elitism and foreignness, in modality and content, of the subtitles. In some ways this may point to a rejection (subtitles are too hard, they marker complexity and pretension) but it also points to an embrace of subtitling as a complex art that can be consumed by large audiences, who may be able to perceive that it is an art which works on the hairline cracks of cultural and sexual difference, revealing these differences rather than domesticating or neutering them. The comedy of subtitles (their mistakes, their perceived elitism, their markering of misunderstanding) may be their locus of power in that these faults inscribe the fictional and real differences we encounter as humans. In this way, I would argue, Allen and Myers do use forms of abusive subtitling as Nornes defines it: they use 'textual and graphic abuse', they experiment 'with language and its grammatical, morphological, and visual qualities – to bring the fact of translation from its position of obscurity'. They critique racial and sexual typologies and stereotypes intralingually that turn their films, even momentarily, 'into *an experience of translation*'.[36] Rather than being an obscure art that seems to fetishize our fear of the other, we may find in these films that subtitling is more of a quotidian necessity even within one culture. The lovers in *Annie Hall* and *Wayne's World* are all American and they all come from different cultures, a move the filmmakers make perhaps to intensify the sense of sexual otherness and to ask whether, when it comes to love, we all speak a foreign language.

35 Dubino, 'Wayne's World: Postmodern or Nostalgic?', 146. See also *Goldmember* box office figures from: http://www.imdb.com/title/tt0295178/business. Accessed 10 August 2009.

36 Nornes, 'For an Abusive Subtitling', 18.

Bibliography

Adejunmobi, Moradewun, 'Translation and Postcolonial Identity: African Writing and European Languages', *The Translator* 4 (1998), 163–81

Ahlqvist, Anders, ed. and trans., *The Early Irish Linguist: an Edition of the Canonical Part of the Auraicept na n-Éces* (Helsinki: Societas Scientiarum Fennica, 1983)

Anlezark, Daniel, ed. and trans., *The Old English Dialogues of Solomon and Saturn* (Cambridge: Boydell and Brewer, 2007)

Austin, J.L., *How To Do Things With Words*, ed. J.O. Urmson and Marina Sbisà, 2nd edn (London: Oxford University Press, 1976)

Bales, Richard, *Proust: A la recherche du temps perdu* (London, Grant & Cutler, 1995)

Baranczak, Stanislaw, *Breathing Under Water and other East European Essays* (Cambridge, Mass. and London: Harvard University Press, 1990)

Barry, David, '"Sollte der herrliche Sohn uns an der Seite nicht stehn?": Priapus and Goethe's *Römische Elegien*', *Monatshefte* 82 (1990), 421–34

Baumgarten, Rolf, 'The geographical orientation of Ireland in Isidore and Orosius', *Peritia* 3 (1984), 189–203

Beil, Ulrich J., 'Die "verspätete Nation" und ihre Weltliteratur: Deutsche Kanonbildung im 19. und frühen 20. Jahrhundert', in *Kanon, Macht, Kultur: Theoretische, historische und soziale Aspekte ästhetischer Kanonbildungen*, ed. Renate von Heydebrand (Stuttgart: Metzler, 1998), 323–40

Berman, Antoine, *Pour une critique des traductions: John Donne* (Paris: Gallimand, 1995)

Best, Richard and M.A. O'Brien, ed., *The Book of Leinster* vol. 4 (Dublin: Dublin Institute for Advanced Studies, 1965)

Bettelheim, Bruno, *The Informed Heart: The Human Condition in Modern Mass Society* (London, Thames and Hudson, 1961)

Bolger, Dermot, ed., *An Tonn Gheal/ The Bright Wave* (Dublin: Raven Arts Press, 1986)

Booth, Wayne C., *The Rhetoric of Fiction* (Chicago: University of Chicago Press, 1968)

Borchmeyer, Dieter, *Die Weimarer Klassik: Eine Einführung* (Königstein im Taunus: Athenäum, 1980)

Borges, Jorge Luis, 'Pierre Menard, Author of Don Quixote', trans. Anthony Bonner, in *Fictions*, ed. Anthony Kerrigan (London: John Calder, 1965)

Borsje, Jacqueline, 'Demonising the enemy: a study of Congal Cáech', in J.E. Rekdal and A. Ó Corráin, ed., *Proceedings of the Eighth Symposium of Societas Celtologica Nordica* (Uppsala: Uppsala Universitet, 2007)

Bowring, Edgar Alfred, *The Poems of Goethe: translated in the original metres*, 2nd edn (London: George Bell & Sons, 1874)

Brakke, David, *Demons and the Making of the Monk: Spiritual Combat in Early Christianity* (Cambridge Mass.: Harvard University Press, 2006)

Brookshaw, David, and Clive Willis, 'Introduction', *Lusophone Studies* 1(Bristol: Bristol University, 2000)

Bushe, Paddy, *In Ainneoin na gCloch* (Dublin: Coiscéim, 2001)

——, *Counsellor* (Ballinskelligs: Sceilg Press, 1991)

——, *Digging Towards The Light* (Dublin: Dedalus Press, 1994)

——, *Hopkins on Skellig Michael* (Dublin: Dedalus Press, 2001)

——, *Teanga* (Dublin: Coiscéim, 1990)

Bussmann, Hadumod, *Routledge Dictionary of Language and Linguistics*, trans. Gregory Trauth and Kerstin Kazzazi (London: Routledge, 1996)

Butler, Judith, 'Competing Universalities', in *Contingency, Hegemony, Universality: Contemporary Dialogues on the Left*, ed. Judith Butler, Ernesto Laclau and Slavoj Zizek (London: Verso, 2000)

Calder, George, ed. and trans., *Imtheachta Aeniasa/ The Irish Aeneid* (London: Irish Texts Society, 1907)

——, ed. and trans., *Togail na Tebe: the Irish Version of the Thebaid of Statius* (Cambridge: Cambridge University Press, 1922)

Cameron, Deborah, 'Demythologizing Sociolinguistics', in *Ideologies of Language*, ed. John E. Joseph and Talbot J. Taylor (London: Routledge, 1990), 79–93

Carey, John and John T. Koch, *The Celtic Heroic Age*, 4th edn (Aberystwyth: Celtic Studies Publications, 2003)

——, *King of Mysteries: Early Irish Religious Writings* (Dublin: Four Courts Press, 2000)

——, *The Irish National Origin-Legend: Synthetic Pseudohistory*, Quiggin Pamphlets on the Sources of Mediaeval Gaelic History, vol. 1 (Cambridge: Cambridge University Press, 1994)

Carney, James, 'Language and literature to 1169', in *A New History of Ireland Vol. 1: Prehistoric and Early Ireland*, ed. Dáibhí Ó Cróinín (Oxford: Oxford University Press, 2003), 451–510

——, ed. and trans., *The Poems of Blathmac* (London: Irish Texts Society, 1964)

Casanova, Pascale, *La République mondiale des lettres* (Paris: Seuil, 1999)

Charalambides, Kyraikos, *Selected Poems* (Cork: Southword Editions, 2005)
Charles-Edwards, Thomas, *Early Christian Ireland* (Cambridge: Cambridge University Press, 2000)
Chaudenson, Robert, 'Geolinguistics, geopolitics, geostrategy: the case of French', in *Languages in a Globalizing World*, ed. Jacques Maurais and Michael A. Morris (Cambridge: Cambridge University Press, 2003), 291–7
Cheesman, Tom, trans., Johann Wolfgang von Goethe, 'Roman Elegies 1790', *Writing Ulster* 1 (1990–91), 138–41
Chesterman, Andrew, 'A Causal Model for Translation Studies', in *Intercultural Faultlines: Research Models in Translation Studies I*, ed. Maeve Olohan (Manchester: St Jerome, 2000), 15–27
——, *Memes of Translation: The Spread of Ideas in Translation Theory* (Amsterdam: Benjamins, 2000)
——, 'Semiotic Modalities in Translation Causality', *Across Languages and Cultures* 3.2 (2002), 145–58
Clarke, Michael, 'An Irish Achilles and a Greek Cú Chulainn', in *II: Proceedings of the Second International Conference on the Ulster Cycle*, ed. Ruairí Ó hUiginn and Brian Ó Catháin, Ulidia (Maynooth: An Sagart, 2009), 271–84
——, *Flesh and Spirit in the Songs of Homer* (Oxford: Oxford University Press, 1999)
Cronin, Michael, 'Babel Atha Cliath: The Languages of Dublin', *New Hibernia Review* 8.4 (Winter 2004), 9–22
——, *Translating Ireland* (Cork: Cork University Press, 1996)
——, *Translation Goes to the Movies* (London and New York: Routledge, 2009)
Damrosch, David, *What is World Literature?* (Princeton: Princeton University Press, 2003)
De Paor, Louis, *Ag Greadadh Bas sa Reilig* (Indreabhán: Cló Iar-Chonnachta, 2005)
——, *Aimsir Bhreicneach* (Canberra: Leros Press, 1993)
——, Louis, *Próca Solais is Luatha* (Dublin: Coiscéim, 1988)
Denison, Norman, 'Plurilingualism and Translation' in *Theory and Practice of Translation*, ed. Lillebill Grähs, Gustav Korlén and Bertil Malmberg (Bern/Frankfurt/Las Vegas: Peter Lang, 1978)
Dillon, Myles, 'The semantic history of Irish gal "valour; steam"', *Celtica* 8 (1968), 196–200
Doane, A.N., ed., *Genesis A* (Madison, Wisconsin: University of Wisconsin Press 1978)
——, ed., *The Saxon Genesis* (Madison, Wisconsin: University of Wisconsin Press, 1991)

Dolan, Terence, *A Dictionary of Hiberno-English: The Irish Use of English* (Dublin: Gill and Macmillan, 1998)
——, 'Translating Irelands: the English Language in the Irish context', in *The Languages of Ireland*, ed. Michael Cronin and Cormac Ó Cuilleanáin (Dublin: Four Courts Press, 2003)
Driessen, C.M., 'Evidence for *ghelh2, a new Indo-European root', *Journal of Indo-European Studies* 31 (2003), 279–305
Dubino, Jeanne, 'Wayne's World: Postmodern or Nostalgic?', *Popular Culture Review* 6.2 (1995), 145–53
Eckermann, Johann Peter, *Gespräche mit Goethe in den letzten Jahren seines Lebens* (Berlin: Aufbau, 1984)
Eco, Umberto, 'An *Ars Oblivionalis*? Forget It!', trans. Marilyn Migiel, *PMLA* 103.3 (May 1988), 254–61
Edmondstoune, W. and Theodore Matrin, trans., *Poems and Ballads of Goethe* (Edinburgh and London: William Blackwell & Sons, 1859)
Etkind, Efim, *Un Art en crise: Essai de poétique de la traduction poétique* (Lausanne: L'Âge d'Homme, 1982)
Evans, Peter William and Celestino Deleyto, ed., *Terms of Endearment: Hollywood Romantic Comedy of the 1980s and 1990s* (Edinburgh: Edinburgh University Press, 1998)
Fanning, David, *Shostakovich: String Quartet No. 8* (Burlington, Vermont and Aldershot: Ashgate, 2004)
Fay, Laurel, *Shostakovich: A Life* (New York: Oxford University Press, 2000)
Félix, Emanuel, *The Possible Journey: Poems 1965–1992*, trans. John M. Kinsella (Gavea-Brown: Providence, 2002)
Filippula, Markku, The *Grammar of Irish English* (London: Routledge, 1999)
Follett, Westley, *Céli Dé in Ireland* (Cambridge: Boydell and Brewer, 2006)
Fuchs, Anne and Sabine Strümper-Krobb, 'Einleitung: Lawrence Passmores I.D.K.-Problem oder die Leiblichkeit der Gefühle', in *Sentimente, Gefühle, Empfindungen: Zur Geschichte und Literatur des Affektiven von 1770 bis heute*, ed. Anne Fuchs and Sabine Strümper-Krobb (Würzburg: Königshausen & Neumann, 2003), 17–26
Gaffney, Phyllis, '"The achieve of, the mastery of the thing!": Pierre Leyris's verse translations of Gerard Manley Hopkins', in *The Practices of Literary Translation: Constraints and Creativity*, ed. Jean Boase-Beier and Michael Holman (Manchester: St Jerome, 1998), 45–58
Ganahl, Rainer, 'Free Markets: Language, Commodification and Art', in Emily Apter ed., *Translation in a Global Market*, special issue of *Public Culture* 13.1 (Winter 2001), 23–38

Gardner, Howard, *Frames of Mind: The Theory of Multiple Intelligences* (London: Heineman, 1983)
Gardner, W.H., and N.H. MacKenzie, eds, *The Poems of Gerard Manley Hopkins*, 4th edn (Oxford and New York: Oxford University Press, 1970)
Garvin, Tom, *Preventing the Future: why was Ireland so poor for so long* (Dublin: Gill and Macmillan, 2004)
Gaurier, Bruno, trans., *Gerard Manley Hopkins: Poèmes* (Suilly-la-Tour: Le Décaèdre, 2003)
Gentner, Dedre and Susan Goldin-Meadow, eds, *Language in Mind: Advances in the Study of Language and Thought* (Cambridge, Mass.: MIT Press, 2003)
Gibson, William, trans., *The poems of Goethe, consisting of his Ballads and Songs and Miscellaneous Selections* (London: Simpkin Marshall & Co, 1883)
Gill, Christopher, *Personality in Greek Epic, Tragedy and Philosophy* (Oxford: Oxford University Press, 1996)
Gilman, Sander L., *Franz Kafka, the Jewish Patient* (New York and London: Routledge, 1995)
Gneuss, Helmut, 'The Battle of Maldon 89: Byrhtnoth's ofermod again', *Studies in Philology* 73 (1976), 117–37
Godden, Malcolm R. (1992), 'Literary language' in *The Cambridge History of the English Language Volume 1: The Beginnings to 1066*, ed. R.M. Hogg (Cambridge: Cambridge University Press, 1992), 490–534
——, 'Biblical poetry: the Old Testament', in *The Cambridge Companion to Old English Literature*, ed. Malcolm Godden and M. Lapidge (Cambridge: Cambridge University Press, 1991), 206–26
Goethe, Johann Wolfgang von, *Das Problem des Übersetzens*, ed. Hans-Joachim Störig (Darmstadt: Wissenschaftliche Buchgesellschaft, 1973)
——, *Goethe's Works*, vol. vii, Bohn's Standard Library, 1st edn (London: John W. Parker & Son, 1853)
——, *Werke*, Hamburger Ausgabe, ed. Erich Trunz (Munich: Beck, 1981)
Golden, Seán, '"Whose morsel of lips will you bite?": Some Reflections on the Role of Prosody and Genre as Non-verbal Elements in the Translation of Poetry', in *Nonverbal Communication and Translation*, ed. Fernando Poyatos (Amsterdam: Benjamins, 1997), 217–45
Graybill, Mark S., '"Nothing Really Matters": Inauthenticity, Intertextuality, and Rock in Wayne's World', *CEA Critic* 66.2–3 (2004), 39–46
Graziosi, Barbara and Johannes Haubold, 'Homeric Masculinity: HNOPEH and AΓHNOPIH', *Journal of Hellenic Studies* 123 (2003), 60–76

Greene, David and Fergus Kelly, ed. and trans., *The Irish Adam and Eve Story from Saltair na Rann: Vol. 1, Text and Translation* (Dublin: Dublin Institute for Advanced Studies, 1976)

Gregory, Augusta, *The Kiltartan Molière* (Dublin: Maunsel, 1910)

——, *Three Last Plays* (London and New York: Putnam, 1928)

Griffith, Mark, ed., *Judith* (Exeter: Exeter University Press, 1997)

Hall, David, and Roger Ames, *Thinking from the Han* (Albany: State University of New York Press, 1998)

Hamburger, Michael, 'On Translation', *PN Review* 16, 1980

Harris, John R, *Adaptations of Roman Epic in Medieval Ireland* (Lewiston: Edwin Mellon Press, 1998)

Harvey, David, *The Condition of Postmodernity* (Oxford: Blackwell, 1990)

Heaney, Seamus, *Preoccupations: Selected Prose 1968–1978* (London: Faber, 1980)

Hederich, Benjamin, *Gründliches mythologisches Lexikon* (Leipzig: Gleditsch, 1770) [reprint Darmstadt: Wissenschaftliche Buchgesellschaft, 1996]

Helder, Herberto, *Poesia Toda* (Lisbon: Assírio & Alvim, 1990)

Hermans, Theo, ed., *The Manipulation of Literature: Studies in Literary Translation* (London: Croom Helm, 1985)

Hindley, Reg, *The Death of the Irish Language: a qualified obituary* (London and New York: Routledge, 1990)

Hirsch, Foster, *Love, Sex, Death and the Meaning of Life: The Films of Woody Allen* (New York: McGraw Hill, 1981)

Jakobson, Roman, 'Closing Statement: Linguistics and Poetics', in *Style in Language*, ed. Thomas A. Sebeok (Cambridge, Mass.: M.I.T. Press, 1960), 350–77

——, 'Linguistic Aspects of Translation', in *On Translation*, ed. Reuben A. Brower (Cambridge, Mass.: Harvard University Press, 1959), 232–9

Jaski, Bart, '"We are of the Greeks in our origin": new perspectives on the Irish origin legend', *Cambrian Medieval Celtic Studies* 46 (2003), 1–53

Keating, Geoffrey, *Foras Feasa ar Éirinn/ The History of Ireland*, vol. 1, ed. David Comyn (London: Irish Texts Society, 1901)

Kelleher, John V., 'The Táin and the Annals', *Ériu* 22 (1971), 107–27

Kelly, Adrian, *Compulsory Irish: Language and Education in Ireland, 1870s–1970s* (Portland, Oregon: Irish Academic Press, 2000)

Kelly, Fergus, *A Guide to Early Irish Law* (Dublin: Dublin Institute for Advanced Studies, 1988)

Kermode, Frank, 'In the Spirit of Mayhew', *London Review of Books* 24.8 (2002), 11–12

Kiberd, Declan and Gabriel Fitzmaurice, ed., *An Crann faoi Bhláth/ The Flowering Tree* (Dublin: Wolfhound Press, 1991)

Kiberd, Declan, *Synge and the Irish Language*, 2nd edn (Dublin: Gill and Macmillan, 1993)

King, Jason, 'Interculturalism and the Irish Theatre: the Portrayal of Immigrants on the Irish Stage', *The Irish Review* 33 (Spring 2005) 23–39

Krobb, Florian, 'Priapean Pursuits: Translation, World Literature and Goethe's *Roman Elegies*', *Orbis Litterarum* 65.1 (2010), 1–21

Krutnik, Frank, 'Love Lies: Romantic Fabrication in Contemporary Romantic Comedy', in *Terms of Endearment: Hollywood Romantic Comedy of the 1980s and 1990s*, ed. Peter William Evans and Celestino Deleyto (Edinburgh: Edinburgh University Press, 1998)

Laborinho, Ana Paula, 'Da descoberta dos povos ao encontro das línguas: o português como lingual intermediária a Oriente', Available online at http://www.humanismolatino.online.pt/v1/pdd/C003-010.pdf

Lefevere, André, 'Translation: Its Genealogy in the West', in *Translation, History & Culture*, ed. Susan Bassnett and André Lefevere (London: Cassell, 1990), 14–28

——, ed., *Translating Literature: the German Tradition from Luther to Rosenzweig* (Assen: van Gorcum, 1977)

——, *Translation/History/Culture: A Sourcebook* (London: Routledge, 1992)

——, *Western Translation Theory from Herodotus to Nietzsche* (Manchester: St Jerome, 2002)

Lehmann, Ruth, ed., *Fled Dúin na nGéd* (Dublin: Dublin Institute for Advanced Studies, 1964)

Lewis, Philip E., 'The Measure of Translation Effects' in *Difference in Translation*, ed. Joseph F. Graham (Ithaca and London: Cornell University Press, 1985), 31–62

Leyris, Pierre, trans., *Gerard Manley Hopkins: Poèmes*, 3rd edn (Paris: Seuil, 1980)

Lind, L.R., trans. and ed., Johann Wolfgang von Goethe, *Roman Elegies and Venetian Epigrams: A Bilingual Text* (Lawrence: University of Kansas Press, 1974)

Liuzza, R.M., ed., *Old English Literature* (New Haven: Yale University Press, 2002)

——, ed., *The Old English Version of the Gospels, Vol. 1: Text and Introduction* (Oxford: Early English Texts Society, 1994)

——, *The Old English Version of the Gospels, Vol. 2: Commentary* (Oxford: Early English Texts Society, 2000)

Longxi, Zhang, *Mighty Opposites: from Dichotomies to Difference in the Comparative Study of China* (Stanford: Stanford University Press, 1998)

Lozovsky, Natalia, '*The Earth is our Book*': *Geographical Knowledge in the Latin West ca. 400–1000* (Ann Arbor: University of Michigan Press, 2000)

Lucas, Peter J., ed., *Exodus*, 2nd edn (Exeter: Exeter University Press, 1994)

Luke, David, trans., Johann Wolfgang von Goethe, *Erotic Poems* (Oxford: Oxford University Press, 1997) [first published 1988]

Mac Gearailt, Uáitéar 'Togail Troí: an example of translating and editing in medieval Ireland', *Studia Hibernica* 31 (2000/2001), 71–86

——, 'Change and innovation in eleventh-century prose narrative in Irish', in *(Re) Oralisierung*, ed. H.L.C. Tristram (Tübingen: Narr Publikationen, 1996), 443–93

——, 'Togail Troí: ein Vorbild für spätmittelirische catha', in *Übersetzung, Adaptation und Akkulturation im insularen Mittelalter*, ed. H.L.C. Tristram and E. Poppe (Münster: Nodus Publikationen, 1999), 123–39

Mac Giolla Léith, Caoimhín, 'Raiding the Vaults and Poetry's Ascendancy', in Louis de Paor, *Ag Greadadh Bas sa Reilg* (Indreabhán: Cló Iar-Chonnachta, 2005)

Mandelbaum, Allen, trans., *The Divine Comedy of Dante Alighieri*, illustrated Barry Moser (Berkeley and London: University of California Press, 1982)

Matthews, Nicole, *Comic Politics: Gender in Hollywood Comedy After the New Right* (Manchester and New York: Manchester University Press, 2000)

McCone, Kim, 'Greek Keltos and Galatos, Latin Gallus "Gaul"', *Die Sprache* 46 (2006), 94–111

——, *Pagan Past and Christian Present in Early Irish Literature* (Maynooth: An Sagart, 1991)

McLuhan, Marshall, *Understanding Media: The Extensions of Man* (Cambridge Mass.: MIT Press, 1994)

Meschonnic, Henri, *Poétique du traduire* (Paris: Verdier, 1999)

Miles, Brent (forthcoming), *Heroic Saga and the Reception of Latin Epic in Medieval Ireland* (Cambridge: Boydell and Brewer)

Mistry, Rohinton, *A Fine Balance* (London: Faber and Faber, 1996)

——, *Family Matters* (London: Faber and Faber, 2002)

Murdoch, Brian, *The Apocryphal Adam and Eve in Medieval Europe* (Oxford: Oxford University Press, 2009)

——, *The Irish Adam and Eve Story from Saltair na Rann, vol. 2: Commentary* (Dublin: Dublin Institute for Advanced Studies, 1976)

Murray, Kevin, ed., *Translations from Classical Literature: Imtheachta Aeniasa and Stair Ercuil ocus a bás*, Irish Texts Society Subsidiary Series no. 17 (London: Irish Texts Society, 2006)

Nedergaard-Larsen, Birgit, 'Culture-Bound Problems in Subtitling', *Perspectives, Studies in Translatology* 2 (1993), 207–42

New American Bible (Washington, DC: Confraternity of Christian Doctrine, 1970, 1986, 1991). http://www.usccb.org/nab/bible/psalms/psalm137.htm

Ní Mhaonaigh, Máire, 'Classical compositions in medieval Ireland: the literary context', in *Translations from Classical Literature: Imtheachta Aeniasa and Stair Ercuil ocus a bás*, Irish Texts Society Subsidiary Series no. 17, ed. Kevin Murray (London: Irish Texts Society, 2006), 1–19

——, *Brian Boru: Ireland's Greatest King?* (Cirencester: Tempus Publishing, 2007)

Nida, Eugene, 'Principles of Translation as Exemplified by Bible Translating', in *On Translation*, ed. Reuben A. Brower (Cambridge, Mass.: Harvard University Press, 1959), 11–31

Niles, John D., 'Maldon and mythopoesis' [originally published 1994], in *Old English Literature*, ed. R.M. Liuzza (New Haven: Yale University Press, 2002), 445–74

Nornes, Abé Mark, 'For an Abusive Subtitling', *Film Quarterly* 52.3 (Spring 1999), 17–34

Ó Cróinín, Dáibhí, 'Ireland, 400–800', in *A New History of Ireland Vol. 1: Prehistoric and Early Ireland*, ed. Dáibhí Ó Cróinín (Oxford: Oxford University Press, 2003), 182–234

——, 'Writing', in *From the Vikings to the Normans*, ed. Wendy Davies (Oxford: Oxford University Press, 2003), 169–202

——, ed., *A New History of Ireland Vol. 1: Prehistoric and Early Ireland* (Oxford: Oxford University Press, 2003)

O'Keeffe, J.G., ed. and trans., *Buile Shuibhne/ The Adventures of Suibhne Geilt* (London: Irish Texts Society, 1910)

O'Leary, Philip, *The Prose Literature of the Gaelic Revival* (Pennsylvania: Pennsylvania University Press, 1994)

O'Rahilly, Cecile, ed. and trans., *Táin Bó Cuailnge Recension I* (Dublin: Dublin Institute for Advanced Studies, 1976)

Orchard, Andy, 'Conspicuous heroism: Abraham, Prudentius, and the Old English Genesis', in *The Poems of Junius 11: Basic Readings*, ed. R.M. Liuzza (London: Routledge, 2002), 119–36

——, 'Latin and the vernacular languages: the creation of a bilingual textual culture', in *After Rome*, ed. Thomas Charles-Edwards (Oxford: Oxford University Press, 2003), 191–220

——, *Pride and Prodigies: Studies in the Monsters of the Beowulf-Manuscript* (Cambridge: D.S. Brewer, 1995)

Pelsmaekers, Katja and Fred Van Besien, 'Subtitling Irony: *Blackadder* in Dutch', *The Translator* 8.2 (2002), 241–66

Pessanha, Camilo, *Obras de Camilo Pessanha: Clepsidra e Poemas Dispersos*, vol. 1 (Mem Martins: Publicações Europa-America, 1988)

Poppe, Erich, 'Stair Ercuil ocus a Bás – rewriting Hercules in Ireland', in *Translations from Classical Literature: Imtheachta Aeniasa and Stair Ercuil ocus a bás*, ed. Kevin Murray, Irish Texts Society Subsidiary Series no. 17 (London: Irish Texts Society, 2006), 37–68

Rafael, Vicente, *Contracting Colonialism: Translation and Christian Conversion in Tagalog Society under Early Spanish Rule* (Ithaca: Cornell University Press 1988)

Rajagopalan, Kanavillil, 'Emotion and Language Politics: The Brazilian Case', *Journal of Multilingual and Multicultural Development* 25.2–3 (2004), 105–23. Special issue, 'Languages and Emotions: A Crosslinguistic Perspective', ed. Jean-Marc Dewaele and Aneta Pavelenko

Rée, Jonathan, *I See a Voice: Deafness, Language and the Senses, a Philosophical History* (New York: Metropolitan Books, 1999)

Remley, Paul G, *Old English Biblical Verse* (Cambridge: Cambridge University Press, 1996)

Reynolds, Suzanne, *Medieval Reading: Grammar, Rhetoric and the Classical Text* (Cambridge: Cambridge University Press, 1996)

Richter, Michael, 'The personnel of learning in early medieval Ireland' in *Irland und Europa im frühen Mittelalter*, ed. Proinséas Ní Chatháin and Michael Richter (Stuttgart: Klett-Cotta, 1996), 275–308

Ritz, Jean-Georges, trans., *Gerard Manley Hopkins: Poèmes 1862–1868, 1876–1899* (Paris: Aubier Montaigne, 1980)

Robinson, Douglas, *The Translator's Turn* (Baltimore and London: Johns Hopkins University Press, 1991)

Robinson, Fred C., 'God, death and loyalty in the Battle of Maldon' [originally published 1979], in *Old English Literature*, ed. R.M. Liuzza (New Haven: Yale University Press, 2002), 425–44

Rosenstock, Gabriel, *Rogha Dánta* (Indreabhán: Cló Iar-Chonnachta, 2005)

——, *Rogha Rosenstock* (Indreabhán: Cló Iar-Chonnachta, 1994)

Roy, Arundhati, *The God of Small Things* (London: Flamingo, 1997)

Russell, Paul, '"What was best of every language": the early history of the Irish language', in *New History of Ireland Vol. 1: Prehistoric and Early Ireland*, ed. Dáibhí Ó Cróinín (Oxford: Oxford University Press, 2003), 405–50

Saar, Erik and Viveca Novak, *Inside The Wire: A Military Intelligence Soldier's Eyewitness Account of Life at Guantánamo* (New York: Penguin Press, 2005)

Schäffner, Christine, ed., *Translation in a Global Village* (Clevedon: Multilingual Matters, 2000)

Scott, Clive, *Translating Baudelaire* (Exeter: University of Exeter Press, 2000)

Sealy, Douglas, and Tomás Mac Siomóin, ed., *Máirtín Ó Direáin: Tacar Dánta/ Selected Poems* (Athlone: The Goldsmith Press, 1984)
Sheidlower, Jesse T. and Jonathan E. Lighter, 'A Recent Coinage (Not!)', *American Speech* 68.2 (Summer 1993), 213–18
Simeoni, Daniel, 'Translating and Studying Translation: The View from the Agent', *Meta* 40.3 (1995), 445–60
——, 'The Pivotal Status of the Translator's Habitus', *Target* 10.1 (1998), 1–39
Simon, Henry W., and Abraham Veinus, *The Pocket Book of Great Operas* (New York: Pocket Books, 1949)
Sirr, Peter, 'The Translation Muscle', *Poetry Ireland Review* 85 (2005), 71–5
Smith, Peter, ed. and trans., *Three Historical Poems Ascribed to Gilla Cóemáin: a Critical Edition of the Work of an Eleventh-Century Irish Scholar* (Münster: Nodus Publikationen, 2007)
Stanton, Robert, *The Culture of Translation in Anglo-Saxon England* (Cambridge: D.S. Brewer, 2002)
Stokes, Whitley, ed. and trans., *In Cath Catharda, in Irische Texte* IV.2, ed. Whitley Stokes and E.Windisch (Leipzig: S. Hirtzel, 1909)
——, ed. and trans., *Togail Troí 1*, in *Irische Texte* II.1, ed. Whitley Stokes and E.Windisch (Leipzig: S. Hirtzel, 1884), 1–141
——, ed. and trans., *Togail Troí from the Book of Leinster* (Calcutta: privately printed, 1881)
Tannen, Deborah, *You Just Don't Understand: Women and Men in Conversation* (New York: Harper, 2007)
Todd, James Henthorn, ed. and trans., *The Irish Version of the Historia Brittonum of Nennius* (Dublin: Irish Archaeological Society, 1848)
Toury, Gideon, *Descriptive Translation Studies and Beyond* (Amsterdam: Benjamins, 1995)
Tristram, Hildegard L.C. 'The "Cattle-Raid of Cuailnge" in tension and transition between the oral and the written: classical subtexts and narrative heritage', in *Cultural Identity and Cultural Integration: Ireland and Europe in the Early Middle Ages*, ed. Doris Edel (Dublin: Four Courts Press, 1995), 61–81
Tymoczko, Maria and Colin Ireland, 'Language and Tradition in Ireland: Prolegomena', in *Language and Tradition in Ireland: Continuities and Displacements*, ed. Maria Tymoczko and Colin Ireland (Amherst and Boston: University of Massachusetts Press, 2003)
Tymoczko, Maria, *Translation in a Postcolonial Context* (Manchester: St Jerome, 1999)
Ueding, Gerd, *Klassik und Romantik: Deutsche Literatur im Zeitalter der Französischen Revolution 1789–1815* (Munich: Hanser, 1987)

Vaget, Hans Rudolf, 'Self-Censorship and Priapic Inspiration', in *A New History of German Literature*, ed. David Wellerby (Cambridge, Mass.: Harvard University Press, 2004), 424–8

Van Hoof, Henri, *Petite Histoire de la traduction en occident* (Louvain-la-Neuve: Cabay, 1986)

Vandaele, Jeroen, '"Funny Fictions": Francoist Translation Censorship of Two Billy Wilder Films', *The Translator* 8.2 (2002), 267–302

Venuti, Lawrence, *Rethinking Translation* (London: Routledge, 1992)

——, *The Translator's Invisibility: a History of Translation* (London: Routledge, 1995)

——, *The Scandals of Translation: Towards an Ethics of Difference* (London: Routledge, 1998)

——, ed., *The Translation Studies Reader*, 2nd edn (New York and London: Routledge, 2004)

——, 'The difference that translation makes: the translator's unconscious', in *Translation Studies: Perspectives on an Emerging Discipline*, ed. Alessandra Riccardi (Cambridge: Cambridge University Press: 2002), 214–41

Volkov, Solomon, *Testimony: The Memoirs of Dmitri Shostakovich as related to and edited by Solomon Volkov*, trans. Antonina W. Bouis (London: Faber, 1981)

Walker, G.S.M., ed. and trans., *Sancti Columbani Opera* (Dublin: Dublin Institute for Advanced Studies, 1997)

Welch, Robert, *Changing States: Transformations in Modern Irish Writing* (London: Routledge, 1993)

Whincup, Greg, *The Heart of Chinese Poetry: China's Greatest Poems Newly Translated* (New York: Doubleday, 1987)

White, Norman, *Hopkins: A Literary Biography* (Oxford: Clarendon Press, 1992)

Wierzbicka, Anna, *Emotions Across Languages and Cultures: Diversity and Universals* (Cambridge: Cambridge University Press, 1999)

Wormald, Patrick, *The Times of Bede: Studies in Early English Christian Society and its Historian* (Oxford: Blackwell, 2006)

Audio Sources

Itzhak Perlman and Klezmer Conservatory Band perf. *Itzhak Perlman in the Fiddler's House.* New York, Angel Records 1995. Reissued in *Perlman plays Klezmer.* London, EMI Classics, 2006

Naftule Brandwein and Abe Schwartz Orchestra perf. *Klezmer!: Jewish Music From Old World To Our World.* Produced by Henry Sapoznik. Newton New Jersey, Shanachie Entertainment, 2000

Psalm 137, http://cgmusic.org/cghymnal/graham/bytheriversofbabylon.htm and http://www.easyenglish.info/psalms/psalm137-taw.htm

Strauss, Richard, 'Morgen!' (Opus 27 no. 4), English edition of the song by John Bernhoff, 1925 Universal-Edition, reproduced on Wikipedia: http://en.wikipedia.org/wiki/Morgen!_(Richard_Strauss)

Vishnevskaya, Galina and others, Ambrosian Opera Chorus and London Philharmonic Orchestra perf. *Lady Macbeth of Mtsensk.* Conducted by Mstislav Rostropovich. By Dmitri Shostakovich. London, EMI Records, 1990. Accompanying booklet by Dmitri Shostakovich and Alexander Preis, librettists. Transliteration and trans. by Joan Pemberton Smith, 128–9

Woolley, John T. and Gerhard Peters, The American Presidency Project [online]. Santa Barbara, CA. Available at: http://www.presidency.ucsb.edu/ws/?pid=25968

Notes on Contributors

MICHAEL CLARKE is Professor of Classics at the National University of Ireland Galway. After an initial training in Homeric studies, he is now a specialist in historical semantics and in the comparative study of ancient and medieval literatures, especially in Greek, Latin, Irish and English. His main current project is on the reinvention of the legend of the Trojan War in medieval Irish texts.

MICHAEL CRONIN holds a Personal Chair in the Faculty of Humanities and Social Studies, Dublin City University and is the Irish Language Literature Advisor for the Arts Council of Ireland. He is the author of numerous publications on language, society and politics. He is a Member of the Royal Irish Academy.

JOHN KINSELLA is Professor of Spanish at the National University of Ireland Maynooth. He has published many articles and a number of books on Spanish American and Lusophone literatures as well as a number of translations. His most recent book is a translation of the Portuguese writer, Emanuel Félix, into Spanish for Anroart Ediciones, and his translation of the poetry of José Saramago is to appear in Gavea-Brown, Brown University, later this year.

FLORIAN KROBB is Professor of German and, since 2010, Head of School, School of Modern Languages, Literatures and Cultures, National University of Ireland Maynooth. He is the author of several monographs on Jewish literature in German, Schiller and autobiography, among other topics. He has also edited several books and is the author of translations and numerous articles.

CORMAC Ó CUILLEANÁIN is Associate Professor of Italian at Trinity College Dublin. A founder member of the Irish Translators' and Interpreters' Association, he has published and researched on issues in translation, and aspects of medieval Italian literature.

KATHLEEN SHIELDS is a lecturer in French at the National University of Ireland Maynooth. She was senior editor on the *Oxford-Hachette Dictionary* and author of *Gained in Translation: Language, Poetry and Identity in Twentieth-Century Ireland*. She has also published articles on translation and French language issues.

MICHELLE WOODS is Assistant Professor of English at the State University of New York, New Paltz. She is the author of *Translating Milan Kundera* (2006) and the forthcoming books *Censoring Translation: Censorship, Theatre and the Politics of Translation* and *Kafka Translated*.

Index

Achebe, Chinua 116
Allen, Woody 125, 126, 131–6, 143
alterity, *see* otherness
Alxinger, Johann Baptist von 18–19
An Claidheamh Soluis 107
Anglo-Saxon *see* Old English
Anime 129
audience 21, 35, 69, 78, 84, 117, 127–35, 138, 139, 143
Austin, J.L. 71

Babel 4, 17, 32, 123
Baranczak, Stanislaw 72
Bede 31
Beowulf 33–5
Bible 1, 34, 37, 38, 72, 85, 84, 90
bilingual editions 20, 220
Blathmac 38, 42–3
Bourdieu, Pierre 6
Bowring, Edgar Alfred 20, 34
Buile Shuibhne 39–40
Bushe, Paddy 112

Camões, Luis de 57
Carlyle, Thomas 10
catchphrases 127
censorship 14, 83, 129
Cheesman, Tom 27
Chesterman, Andrew 3, 91, 98, 104
Chinese 35, 56, 58–64, 111
Cogadh Gaedhel re Gallaibh 46–7
cognition 2, 3, 4, 6, 8, 9, 68, 87, 92, 94
Costa de Torres, Padre 56
cribs 87, 120
cultural intermediary, 29, 80, 93
cultural systems 27, 43, 55, 104, 122

Dante 67–8
Darwin 72
de Paor, Louis 7, 110, 111, 117–19, 120
de-differentiation 121
Die Horen 10, 19

emotion (and landscape) 60–1
(and language contact) 109, 110
(conceptualization of) 2, 3, 4, 6, 48, 71, 89, 103, 104
(eliciting response in reader) 73, 82–3
(externalization of) 14, 18, 20–1, 24–6, 28, 65, 81
(in East) 60
(in impulse of text) 69, 70–1, 73, 85
(in response to translation) 67, 75, 77–9, 136
(in West) 17, 65
English (and Irish) 7, 108–10, 112–21
(in subtitling) 125, 129, 130, 131, 134, 137
(tradition) 32, 33, 37, 44
(translations) 4, 5, 15, 20–1, 24–7, 64, 65, 75, 89, 95, 96, 98, 99, 102
(vocabulary of emotion) 3, 71
eroticism 4, 15, 16, 19–24, 28, 136
Estado da India 57
Etkind, Ephim 91
exceptionalism 115
Exodus 34, 35
extra-textual meaning 70, 71, 79

Félix, Emanuel, 5, 60, 63, 64, 66
film 7, 71, 125, 127–9, 130, 133, 134, 137, 139, 143
Fled Dún na nGéd 52
formalism 89, 101
French 6, 12, 61, 89, 95, 96, 99, 100, 101, 102, 117, 123, 129

Gaelic revival 108
Gaurier, Bruno 95, 96, 88, 100, 102, 105
genderlect 127
Genesis 33, 35–7, 40
German 11, 13, 14, 16, 24, 74, 91, 112, 123
gesture 5, 17, 71, 72
globalization 7, 92, 112, 115, 117, 122, 123
Greek 11, 13, 24, 32, 49, 53, 121
Guantánamo 29, 79–80

habitus 6
Hamburger, Michael 64
Heaney, Seamus 97, 98
heart-mind 5, 61, 64
Hederich 22
Helder, Herberto 60, 66
Hermans, Theo 1, 104
heroic narrative 5, 32, 34, 37, 44, 45, 47, 49, 50, 51, 53
Hiberno-English 7, 109–10, 114–15, 123
Hölderlin 90
hybridization 112, 114–15, 116, 121–2
Hyde, Douglas 109–10, 113–15

Iliad 53
Innti 111
interpreter 13, 27, 25, 65, 68–70, 79–81
Ireland, Colin 122
Irish (ancient) 51, 110
(modern) 7, 107–22
(old and middle) 3, 4, 5, 31
Irish Aeneid 51–2
Isidore of Seville 31
Italian 68, 78
Italian Journey 15

Jail Journal 108
Jakobson, Roman 68–9, 73
Japanese 60, 63, 129, 141
Jesuits 55–7
Judith 33–4

Kiberd, Declan 109, 115
kinaesthetic intelligence 88–9, 98
King, Martin Luther 5, 78–9, 82
Klezmer tradition 5, 77–8

Lambert, José 104
Latin 11, 21–3, 32, 34, 36, 38, 39, 40, 41, 44, 45, 46, 49, 51, 52, 53, 57, 65
Lebor Gabála 31–2, 45
Lefevere, André 91
Leyris, Pierre 87, 94–5, 100
Lind, L.R. 27
literati 30–1, 46, 53
Lucan 46, 50
Luís Fróis 55
Luke, David 20–1, 23, 25–7

Meschonnic, Henri 4, 92
Mistry, Rohinton 116
monolingual speakers 125, 127
multiculturalism 7
multilingualism 7, 29, 114–15, 121
music 17, 69, 73–8, 89, 98, 101, 102, 137
Myers, Mike 126, 140–1, 142, 143

Napoleon 12–13
national literature 10–12, 15, 45, 101, 107, 108, 110
Nida, Eugene A. 72

Nixon, Richard 82
Nornes, Abé Mark 126, 128–9, 135, 140, 143

Ó Conaire, Pádraig 108
Ó Donnchadha, Tadhg 107
opera 5, 73, 74, 76, 77
oral language 44, 71, 97, 98
Orosius 31
otherness 2, 16, 18, 56, 57, 58, 62, 64, 66, 110, 113, 115, 116, 117, 119, 128, 133, 141, 142, 143

Pearse, Pádraig 108
performance 3, 4, 67, 69, 70, 75, 76, 78, 88, 92
Pessanha, Camilo 62
phonetics 64, 65, 68, 74, 78, 88, 89, 90, 93, 96, 97, 100, 101, 102, 103, 105, 113, 137
pidgin 116
plurilingualism, *see* multilingualism
poetry 5, 14, 16, 17, 20, 33, 53, 58, 59, 62, 99, 111, 112
Portuguese 2, 3, 5, 56, 59, 60, 63, 64, 65, 117
postmodern 126, 137
Pravda 76–7
preconscious 93–4, 97–8
pre-literate 6, 98, 105, 95, 97, 98, 99, 105
Propertius 19
prosody 6, 88–9, 100–1, 104
Proust 69
psalms 5, 33, 83–4, 92
puns 6, 87, 92, 99, 100, 105, 113, 119, 129

register 25–7, 45, 130–3, 138
Ritz, Jean-Georges 87, 95
Robinson, Douglas 1, 90–2
Romanticism 4, 89, 91, 102
Rosenstock, Gabriel 7, 110–12, 115, 117, 121
Roy, Arundhati 116
Russian 75

Saltair na Rann 38–43
Schiller 10
Schleiermacher 11, 90
Scott, Clive 89, 101
semantic content 2, 3, 9, 49, 65, 72, 89–93, 100, 101, 104
Shostakovich 5, 75–6
Simeoni, Daniel 2, 6, 9
socio-ethnic difference 7, 127
sociolinguistics 103
song 5, 33, 60, 67, 83, 93, 98, 102, 113, 114
source text 1, 5, 27–9, 39, 41, 44, 45, 67, 73, 79, 87, 99, 100–1, 113, 117–18, 121
Spanish 59, 113
sprung rhythm 98–102
strategies (in translating) 3, 32, 94, 110, 115, 129
  (domesticating) 114, 143
  (foreignizing) 113, 120, 123, 128
subtitling (abusive) 125, 128–9
  (and culture-bound texts) 127, 129
  (and foreignness) 143

Thirty Years War 12
Toury, Gideon 1, 94, 98, 104
translation (approaches to) 4, 9, 11, 28, 70, 89, 90, 98, 101, 104, 108, 120
  (as activity) 3, 4, 67, 69–70, 78, 92
  (as trope) 2, 7, 8, 48, 136, 143
  (first) 65
  (interlingual) 5, 69, 71, 74, 127, 129
  (intersemiotic) 5, 71, 73, 74
  (intralingual) 5, 7, 143
  (models) 3, 59, 79, 91, 103, 125
  (multiple versions) 21, 84–5, 95

translation studies 1, 4, 6, 87–91, 101–5
translator 1, 2, 28, 104–5, 107
(duty) 5, 73, 85, 102, 128
(emotions) 3, 5, 64
(error) 70, 93, 113
(mediator) 15, 23, 24, 29, 58, 59, 65, 93, 112–13
(modesty) 24, 29, 100, 104
(performer, writer) 4, 5, 63, 73, 95
(roles) 5, 79–81
(subjectivity) 3, 6, 67–8, 90–1, 93, 97, 103
(thought processes) 3, 70, 98
(training) 4, 6, 94–8, 100, 104
(visibility) 140
translingualism 9, 116, 121
Tymoczko, Maria 2, 122

Venuti, Lawrence 93, 98, 116, 128

Welch, Robert 111–12, 122
Welsh 98, 107
Weltliteratur 4, 9–13, 15, 19, 28
(and world poetry) 58, 111
Whorf, Benjamin 29
written word 71

Zhang Longxi 58–9

Intercultural Studies and Foreign Language Learning

SERIES EDITORS
Arnd Witte and Theo Harden

Learning a foreign language facilitates the most intimate access one can get to the culture and society of another language community. The process of learning a foreign language always involves intercultural levels of engagement between the languages and cultures concerned. This process is also a long and tedious one which involves an enormous variety of factors. These factors are located on individual, socio-cultural and linguistic planes. They engage in a complex interplay between any elements of these more general planes and the concrete learning process of the learner.

The series *Intercultural Studies and Foreign Language Learning* is intended to provide a forum for publishing research in this area. It will publish monographs, edited collections and volumes of primary material on any aspect of intercultural research. The series is not limited to the field of applied linguistics but it will also include relevant research from linguistic anthropology, language learning pedagogy, translation studies and language philosophy.

The series editors are Dr Arnd Witte, who can be contacted by emailing a.witte@nuim.ie, and Prof Theo Harden, theo.harden@ucd.ie.

Vol. 1 Freda Mishan and Angela Chambers (eds):
Perspectives on Language Learning Materials Development.
294 pages. 2010. ISBN: 978-3-03911-863-2

Vol. 2 Valerie Pellatt, Kate Griffiths and Shao-Chuan Wu (eds):
Teaching and Testing Interpreting and Translating.
343 pages. 2010. ISBN: 978-3-03911-892-2

Vol. 3 Arnd Witte, Theo Harden and Alessandra Ramos de Oliveira Harden (eds): Translation in Second Language Learning and Teaching.
424 pages. 2009. ISBN: 978-3-03911-897-7

Vol 4 Kathleen Shields and Michael Clarke (eds): Translating Emotion: Studies in Transformation and Renewal Between Languages.
172 pages. 2011. ISBN: 978-3-0343-0115-2

Vol. 5 Jane Fenoulhet and Cristina Ros i Solé (eds): Mobility and Localisation in Language Learning: A View from Languages of the Wider World.
253 pages. 2011. ISBN: 978-3-0343-0150-3

Vol. 6 Forthcoming

Vol. 7 Michael Hager: Culture, Psychology, and Language Learning.
358 pages. 2011. ISBN: 978-3-0343-0197-8